The Cloud and the Silver Lining

The Cloud
and the
Silver Lining

Ezekiel, the Christian and the Power of God

Denis Lane

 EVANGELICAL PRESS

EVANGELICAL PRESS,
16/18, High Street, Welwyn, Herts, AL6 9EQ, England.

© Evangelical Press 1985
First published 1985

ISBN 0 85234 193 8

Published jointly by Evangelical Press and OMF Books.

Bible quotations are from the New International Version,
Hodder and Stoughton, 1979

Typeset by Inset, Chappel, Essex
Printed in Great Britain by Cox and Wyman, Reading, Berks.

Contents

The vision

1.
A vision of God

The man had hit bottom. Everything had gone wrong with his life. For five years he had been an exile, one of that army of forced refugees with which our day and age are only too familiar. Now, at thirty years of age, he had graduated to unemployment. His education and family training had prepared him for the office of a priest, and you had to be thirty to qualify for the job. But how can you be a priest without a sanctuary? For the last five years the temple in Jerusalem had been for him a distant relic of a receding past. Life might have been more encouraging if the other exiles had shown some spiritual desires, but they seemed settled in apathy and drugged by despair, caught in a careless cultural sterility. As for God, he was the remote one, the sealer of their fate, the determiner of their destiny, impotent in the face of Babylonian military might and far removed from the dreary realities of the refugee camp.

World circumstances did nothing to lift Ezekiel's spirits. He lived in a time of recurrent Middle East crises. His own nation of Judah was still surviving in remnant form, deprived of the cream of her leadership and living in constant fear of invasion and extinction. The life had gone out of her ancient faith and the commitment of her people to the Lord was half-hearted, more and more syncretistic and almost totally irrelevant to daily life. Muggings were frequent throughout Judah, bribery and corruption scandals often rocked the establishment and in the middle of it all a self-satisfied church parroted

clichés and echoed the world's latest humanistic theories.
'There will always be a Judah,' seemed the main theme
of their songs, for, of course, God would never allow his
temple to be desecrated and they had always muddled
through before. To the exiled refugee across in Babylon
the self-satisfied optimism of his homeland had the same
hollow ring as Western humanistic contentment had to
Solzhenitzyn when he emerged from Russia.

At such a time and in such circumstances God broke
in, bringing a renewed vision and a clear message to the
man who felt he could never be any more use. What to
man is the end, to God was the beginning of something
new. A concealed door suddenly appeared in the blank
wall in front of him, inviting him to push through. Out
of the very darkness of the scenery emerged a new and
bright light.

The message of the cloud (1: 1–9)

For Ezekiel the first impression was of total darkness.
We may picture him wandering out of the camp by the river
Kebar and looking with horror at the black clouds lowering
over the northern horizon, growing more threatening by
the minute. Those clouds from that direction spoke only
too clearly of the threat of invasion from the north hanging
over his homeland, an omen of imminent destruction. Like
the mushroom cloud looming over civilization in our day,
those clouds spoke of inescapable doom. But out of the
storm came a vision.

I do not profess to know exactly what happened to
Ezekiel and whether the vision he saw was in a kind of
trance or in the inner recesses of his mind. Our generation
is obsessed with how things happen, but what is usually
more important is who causes them to happen and why.
I have no doubt that God caused Ezekiel to see what he

saw and that he did so for the instruction of Ezekiel's generation and ours. And Ezekiel saw light in the midst of darkness. The cloud was not the end, as 1:4 indicates. Around the cloud ran a silver lining, visible evidence that while the cloud might temporarily obscure the sun, it did not extinguish it. Behind and beyond the cloud the sun shone just as brightly as ever. The truth began to dawn on Ezekiel that it takes more than personal, social or political crises to overcome God's rule of his world.

Some years ago I was visiting Laos, and as we sat together in the evening, the silence of the tropical night was suddenly shattered by violent noise. Guns popped, saucepan lids clashed, voices yelled and all the chaos of a riot or revolution burst around us. We went out to see what had happened, only to discover that the eclipse of the moon was responsible. The next day a local helper told us how disappointed they had been the previous evening because, despite all the noise, the 'frog managed to swallow the moon'. 'But it was all right in the end,' she went on, 'because the moon came out the other side.' We may smile at her beliefs, but we often behave as though light has been swallowed by darkness and God has been devoured by our circumstances. Ezekiel had to be reminded that the eternal and almighty God is not easily obliterated by crises, however dark they seem from our side.

That was not all. From within the cloud lightning flashed and in the centre of the cloud Ezekiel saw an intense fire burning, symbol of the holiness and burning purity of the God whom he served. God was at work in the midst of the cloud and from it his servants emerged. In fact this vision was more about the servants of God and the throne of God than about God himself. Beginning with that depressing cloud of threatening catastrophe, God took Ezekiel through scenes of his angelic forces, on to the divine chariot of his mobility and then up to

the throne of his transcendence. Ezekiel was too pre-
occupied with his problems for God to begin with the
throne, and the man in need had to learn that the God
he felt to be far away and unconcerned was in fact inti-
mately at work in the very middle of the cloud that
threatened him. God is the God in whom we live and
move and have our being, and not just the God 'out
there'. Ezekiel needed to feel that as well as to know
it with his head.

One of the difficulties in describing a vision of God
or of spiritual realities is the limitation of human
experience and language. We can only describe things
in the language with which we are familiar, but human
language does not normally deal with divine or spiritual
reality. Therefore we have to express such matters in
the nearest language we have, which inevitably involves
human   or   anthropomorphic   expressions.   Ezekiel
struggled with this inadequacy and frequently used such
phrases as 'the appearance of', 'the likeness of', 'it looked
like', or 'like the appearance of'. The nearer the vision
drew to the throne of God, the more these phrases were
used. This should not put us off attempting to see what
God was saying in the vision. While we do not want to
indulge in fanciful allegory, we have to recognize the
picture language being used and can legitimately ask ourselves what God was seeking to convey to his servant.

The message of the servants (1: 10–14)

The angelic servants of the Lord came from the burning
fire of the holy presence of the living God. They had
human characteristics, indicating the high place given to
man in creation. While they had wings to fly in the
execution of God's purposes, they also had the hands of
a man to serve (1:8). They were in constant touch with

each other and moved straight ahead in obedience to the Spirit, without turning in the least from their allotted positions and assignments. As with other visions of angels and particularly of cherubim in Scripture, they had four faces, portraying the intelligence of a man, the boldness of a lion, the strength of an ox and the soaring qualities of an eagle. They themselves evinced the burning quality of the fire from which they came and moved to the execution of their work with the speed of lightning.

Ezekiel needed to realize that, while on earth nothing seemed to be happening, in the councils of heaven God was fully active and carrying out his purposes in the world. The angelic servants of God were not idle and God himself had not relinquished either his interest or his power, despite the evidence to the contrary. Periods when God seems inactive upon earth must not be misinterpreted, either by believers or unbelievers, as meaning that God has relaxed his government of the universe. There is a rhythm to life that calls for times of quietness as well as times of intense activity. Spiritual life seems to show this characteristic too, and while we must not be content with apathy and carelessness, neither must we assume that when nothing seems to be moving on the surface, God has ceased to care.

The message of the wheels (1: 15—21)

Ezekiel then saw a vehicle that must have reminded him immediately of the chariots of war so familiar in military parades in Babylon. Those dreaded tanks of the ancient world had rolled across the Middle East, destroying armies before them and eventually reducing his own country to submission and dependency. Judah could not boast such armaments. When he had first arrived in Babylon, Ezekiel must have been shocked by the sheer size of the place,

the magnificence of its buildings and the might of its
armies. Jerusalem and Judah, which from his youth he
had seen as the centre of the universe and the dwelling-
place of the Lord of all creation, must have seemed minute
and insignificant by comparison. Doubts had probably
flooded his mind. Was God so great after all? Had he
been misled by the insular nature of his own homeland,
unaware of the big world beyond? Had not Babylon and
its gods proved more than a match for the Lord and his
hosts?

Here in the vision was God's answer. The armies of the
living God do indeed have chariots, mighty weapons of
war, but their armaments are spiritual, not fleshly, and
they must be seen by faith. In fact, in the vision the throne
of God was mounted above the chariot, and the message
comes clearly through that Israel's God is fully mobile
and fully able to cope with every situation.

God reveals himself to his people according to their
needs at particular times in history. In Isaiah 6 we are
told how the prophet saw the Lord high and lifted up
and filling the temple. King Uzziah had just died after a
fifty-year reign, and at that time Isaiah and Israel needed
to know that God was still among them, reigning supreme
and settled among his people and in his dwelling. Despite
the threats from other countries, God still intended to
bless Judah in Jerusalem. Such a message, however, would
have had no relevance for Ezekiel. He was hundreds of
miles away from the temple and the country, and his
very fear was that God's power did not reach to Babylon.
So God revealed himself to his servant as the mobile one,
riding upon a heavenly chariot, not one bit less powerful
than all the tanks of Babylon.

Beside each creature in the vision stood a remarkable
wheel, the like of which man has not yet invented. It was
on the ground, indicating that God was totally in touch
with what was happening. Each wheel was intersected at

right angles by another wheel, enabling the chariot to move backwards, forwards or sideways without any trouble. So God's throne could move in any direction at any instant, with the speed of lightning, yet still the wheels appeared not to turn. Here was 'deliberate speed, majestic instancy' of the kind portrayed by Francis Thompson in his poem *The Hound of Heaven*. The rims of the wheels were 'high and awesome'. Any infantryman in an ancient army must have been appalled to see the great wheels of enemy chariots rolling down on him, looming above him before they struck; the same sense of awe came across to Ezekiel. The fact that the rims of the wheels were 'full of eyes all around' confirmed that God knew all that was going on upon the earth. The wheels themselves were somehow living, for the 'spirit of the living creatures was in the wheels'. As one being, the angelic beings and the chariot itself moved in perfect harmony and majestic unity, and the whole was capable of rising from the earth like some modern space vehicle.

Nothing could have spoken more eloquently to Ezekiel about the greatness of the God of Judah and his undoubted capacity to deal with the military forces of the day and the crushing events that had so overwhelmed the spirit of the prophet. Once again Ezekiel was made to feel the greatness of God and to grasp it afresh with his mind. Even the loss of the temple and of Jerusalem could have no real effect upon such a God. Moving without changing, he could as truly be with the exiles in their camps as with the survivors in their city. Nothing could happen without his knowledge or permission.

The message of the throne (1: 25—28)

Turning his attention to the living creatures again, Ezekiel noticed their wings stretched out towards each other and

he was made forcibly aware of their movement by the
noise they created. 'Like the roar of rushing waters, like
the voice of the Almighty, like the tumult of an army,'
is how he described it (1:24). Babylon's battalions shrank
to insignificance before the hosts of God.

The sight and sound of those angelic wings led Ezekiel's
eyes to the vast expanse of heaven spread out above them,
'sparkling like ice and awesome' (1:22). That expanse
and its position above the warring hosts conveyed a message
of timeless infinity and shrank man's earthly strivings and
puny achievements to the size of a speck of dust. Like a
single man in a boat surrounded by the endless waste of a
limitless ocean, or a lost traveller in the Sahara smitten
by the loneliness of humanity in a featureless world,
Ezekiel was made to feel his true position before his
Creator.

At times the angelic beings stood still and, as they did
so, they lowered their wings. Unlike some of God's servants
on earth, they did not suffer from the illusion that if their
particular wings were allowed to rest for a moment, the
throne of heaven would come crashing down. In fact, it
was at the very time when they lowered their wings and
the noise stopped, that the voice of God could be heard
floating across the vast expanse and calling Ezekiel's
attention to the throne above.

Strange to say, the throne was in some ways the least
awe-inspiring aspect of the vision, for although it was
brilliant with the blue of the sapphire or the brightness
of the sky, the figure on the throne was 'a figure like that
of a man'. What could speak more strongly of man being
made in the image of God, and of God understanding the
feelings of his people? For us who know the incarnation,
death, resurrection and ascension of our Lord Jesus Christ
the message is even clearer, for he has taken his humanity
with him to the very throne of God, and there he reigns
until all his enemies become his footstool.

The figure on the throne was no soft and weak carica-
ture, nor was he the kindly grandfather figure of the 'man
upstairs' that so many modern people imagine God to be.
From his waist up he was all fire, and from there downwards 'he looked like fire; and brilliant light surrounded
him'. The holiness of God burned through the scene.
Even so, the final touch to the picture of the throne was
a surrounding rainbow. Reminder of God's covenant to
Noah, the rainbow spoke of grace in the midst of judgement, love in the centre of holiness and concern in the
presence of catastrophe.

Ezekiel had seen a fresh view of God, in close and
intimate contact with the events of earth, constantly
active when nothing seemed to be happening, completely
able to cope with the latest crises of humanity, reigning
in holy transcendence upon the throne of the universe,
far above the wars and tumults that afflict the human
race, yet personal in his concern, gracious in his holiness
and by no means the absentee God. Wars could dissolve
continents, monetary systems might collapse, earthquakes
could shatter cities and man might pollute his way across
the lands and oceans of the world, but God was still and
is still in control.

At the sight of such a God, as he felt the impact of
this vision upon his soul, Ezekiel could only fall on his
face in humility, awe and worship. And that is the very
position we modern men and women find most difficult
to adopt. Drunk with the wine of our own achievements,
glorying in the multitude of our new discoveries, deluged
by the tide of our technology, we tend to feel, as Ezekiel
had felt, that this new Babylon is a very wonderful place,
and perhaps the God of our fathers was a little exaggerated.
We do not find room in our universe for God, because we
think we can explain it all.

That is understandable in the unbelieving world, but
the most disturbing aspect is that believers have lost the

vision, too, and as J. B. Phillips put it, 'Your God is too
small'. Revival has always been accompanied, even if not
always begun, by a renewed sense of the holy transcendence and majesty of God. When people have not only
believed, but felt and seen the greatness and glory of the
invisible, incorruptible God, and have been so moved by
what they have seen that they have been prostrated before
him, new hope has been born. No generation needed such
experiences more than ours does.

2.
A message from God

In the last few years, movements within the churches
have brought a renewed emphasis on the supernatural and
the miraculous. No longer is it thought strange for God
to grant visions to men and women and to lead them
directly by his Spirit. The pendulum has swung strongly
in the direction of the experiential, after a period when
evangelical Christianity had become excessively intellectual. Over-emphasis on one side of spiritual truth inevitably results in this strong swing back, often to another
extreme, until by the grace of God some new balance
is reached. People had been taught that feelings were
not necessary to faith, and excessive reliance had been
placed on the bare word of Scripture as the sole ground
of assurance and confidence. The reaction to this has
sometimes tended to emphasize the importance of sub-
jective experience so much that the content of the Word
of God seems to be missing.

The early chapters of Ezekiel speak of the need for a
clear vision of God, a warm and living experience of him,
and yet at the same time for a strong understanding of
what he is saying through his Word to the present
generation. In Ezekiel's situation he desperately needed
an injection of confidence in the reality of God, and
the kind of new assurance of his greatness that only the
vision could produce. He was to be a lone voice in the
middle of a babel of opposition, the only one in step with
God, when the whole community seemed to be marching
to another tune. He could not do this without being sure

in the depths of his being of the ground on which he stood. Yet the Lord also brought to him the Word of God, a strong message with clear rational content, speaking in no uncertain terms to the needs of the contemporary world. So in 1:1 Ezekiel is said to have seen 'visions of God', and in 1:3 'the word of the Lord came to' him.

This is the pattern right through Scripture. Every time God granted a renewed vision of himself to some person, he also gave him a message to communicate to those around. What God has joined together we must not put asunder: warm, living experience and cool rational understanding belong together in the purposes of God.

We left Ezekiel lying flat on his face before God, struck down in awe at the vision of the greatness of his Lord. Yet he was also aware that God was speaking to him. We might think that God in his greatness would wish to leave this man lying upon the ground, while he passed on his word to him. But that is not God's way. He recognizes the need for awe and worship and the rightful position of creatures before their Creator, but he also wishes to impart to them that sense of dignity that follows from accepting their true position before him. So the Lord told Ezekiel to stand on his feet, and by his Holy Spirit gave him the power to do so. Once man sees his real weakness, the Lord is ready to impart his power. The self-sufficient and the proud are the ones who know nothing of worship and nothing of spiritual strengthening, and thereby shut themselves off from hearing the voice of God.

When the Lord began speaking, he did not ask for volunteers for his work. In fact he left Ezekiel with no real choice. 'Son of man, *I am sending you* to the Israelites' (2:3). Once man has seen his real position before the Lord, he can only bow his head and obey. We do not do God a favour by serving him. Sometimes God does work by asking for volunteers, as in Isaiah 6, when the prophet saw the need and responded to God's question: 'Who will go for us?' On other occasions he simply commands, particularly at crucial times in the history of a people. Ezekiel lived in such a time.

The people to whom he was sent

The prospect offered to Ezekiel was a daunting one, for he was sent to a nation of rebels. Historically they had that reputation, and they still deserved it (2:3). They were obstinate and stubborn (2:4). No doubt they would have called themselves strong-minded! Living among them would be like camping in a thorn bush and staying among scorpions (2:6). These people might listen or fail to listen, but Ezekiel still had to go and tell them God's message. In fact, he was warned that they would not be willing to listen to him, simply because they were not willing to listen to God.

There was certainly very little of the 'romance' of preaching in Ezekiel's life. Nor was he promised that if he followed all the rules he would be successful. In fact, rather like Isaiah before him and, indeed, like many of God's choicest servants, he was promised a hard path with little affirmation and much opposition. He was there to proclaim the message of the Word of God, whether people wanted to hear it or not. What was important was that the people should know 'that a prophet has been among them' (2:5). This did not allow him to adopt a take-it-or-leave-it mentality, but rather it called for willingness to utter a message that his generation considered unacceptable. In a day like Ezekiel's, or ours, when people want to hear what they want to hear, few are prepared to challenge them with the contrary standards of God's Word. Only a person who has seen God in his holiness is likely to be able to do so.

In recent years we have learned many things about

presenting the gospel in a form that begins with people's felt needs — about 'scratching where it itches'. Taken too far, this approach reduces the gospel to a plaster to cover men's wounds and reduces God to a new God of the gaps; not this time the gaps in scientific knowledge, but the gaps in human self-sufficiency. We need to relearn that God the sovereign Creator summons men to respond to him: he is not simply there to respond to their summons for help. If he were, then the strong would not need him, as indeed they themselves say, 'I do not need your gospel to help me in my need. I can manage without crutches.' Therefore we must recapture like Ezekiel our sense of God's majesty and of our message being 'what the Sovereign Lord says . . . whether they listen or fail to listen'.

The opposition he must expect

Israel not only failed to listen to God's Word to them, but positively rejected it. Ezekiel was told not to be afraid of what they said or terrified by them (2:6). Quite clearly the opposition was organized and vocal. Pressure groups considered the straightforward religion of the Lord as a relic of an ancient past. New, more liberal attitudes towards religion and morals not only pervaded the lives of individuals but were entrenched in organized groups. In fact, God told Ezekiel that he would have stood a better chance of a hearing if he had been sent to foreign peoples whose language he could not understand.

In the modern Western world, where Christianity is popularly regarded as the religion of the past and the church as a dying institution, bound by the chains of tradition and insensitive to the needs around, similar attitudes prevail. Secularized society accepts without question the autonomy of the individual and freedom for anything as a basic right. Opposition to Christian viewpoints, whether on the origin of the universe, sexual morality, the sanctity of human life, the equality of all men in God's sight or the emptiness of materialism, take a daily beating. The Christian consensus that once under-girded society no longer exists to put a brake on agress-ive salesmen for any and every new way. Militants of every kind flourish. Those who stand against such groups can easily be intimidated by looks and words and violent opposition. The person with a vision of God and a word from him must hold no illusions about the battle that lies before him.

The equipment he was given

Israel was hardened and obstinate, but the man of God could not give ground. Aggressive rebellion against the ways and will of God had to be met by unshakeable faith and obedience. God told Ezekiel, 'I will make you as unyielding and hardened as they are. I will make your forehead like the hardest stone, harder than flint' (3:9). I do not know how sensitive Ezekiel's temperament was, but most people shrink back from confrontation. Certainly some Christians seem to thrive on it, but usually that is because of some insecurity in their back-ground that sends them out fighting from their corner. Most people find controversy distasteful, yet at times it is necessary, and at such times God equips even his most timid saints with the boldness they require.

Hard-heartedness in Israel more than met its match in Ezekiel's hard-headedness. Disobedience clothed as freedom was stripped of its disguise. The church of his day might be yielding ground all along the way, but Ezekiel was given the toughness of mind to take a stand beyond which he would not yield. We are never told he

became hard-hearted and his later tears for Israel's sorrows
indicate that he never did, but tough-mindedness was
another matter. In our day we need that same equipment
to stand firm on truth and morals, for tolerance has in
some cases become the overriding virtue, extending not
only to doctrinal error, but also to immorality. Someone has to say, 'The rot stops here.'

The message he was given to digest

Ezekiel was not allowed the luxury of feeling that he was
different from the rest of his contemporaries. He too was
a son of man, fully human on every count. He was warned
that he needed to listen to the Word of God himself first.
He was not to rebel like the rebellious house of Israel
(2:8), but to digest God's message and make it a part of
himself. That involved a response in his own heart and
mind.

The message was not easy either, for the roll on which
it was written was covered with script on both sides, and
the words were full of lamentation and mourning and
woe (2:8—10). No one likes to be a bearer of bad news,
but sometimes bad news must precede the good. To carry
bad news in an acceptable manner requires wisdom and
tact, and to preach a message of judgement on sin requires
unusual spiritual sensitivity. No wonder Ezekiel needed
the empowering of God. In any society that is falling apart,
God's message inevitably begins with some bad news about
the causes of the disintegration, and unless God's people
are prepared to present that aspect of truth faithfully
they cannot expect to see real changes.

On the other hand, paradoxically, when Ezekiel filled
his stomach with the scroll containing the message of
judgement, we are told that 'it tasted as sweet as honey
in my mouth'. When we are in line with the will of God,

the most difficult task can become acceptable. Peace comes from boldly taking whatever God gives to us and faithfully discharging our responsibility, not from avoiding the issue and refusing to grasp the nettle.

The responsibility he had to bear

The solemn nature of this responsibility was emphasized for Ezekiel after a further seven days, days no doubt in which he spent time meditating on what he had seen and heard. The word of the Lord came to him again, making him a watchman for his people and warning him that he would be held responsible, not for the reaction of people to his ministry, but for faithful deliverance of the message. He was called to be responsible to God and *to* the people, but he was not held responsible *for* the people in their handling of what they heard. Some would hear and respond and be saved. Others would not turn from their sin and would die. What he had to do was to present the truth.

Once he had warned the wicked man and alerted him to the inevitable result of his ways, Ezekiel's responsibility was discharged. He needed to use persuasion, or rather dissuasion from evil, but having done so, he passed the responsibility on to the man himself.

God's people in every generation stand as watchmen to their society and its people, warning them of the consequences of apostasy and immorality. This role is often left to a few concerned individuals, but if the community has lost its voice, someone has to speak out. The responsibility is real and God holds us to account if we fail. When we say nothing in a day of danger, we are culpable.

When on the first Easter Day the Lord commissioned his disciples he said, ' "As the Father has sent me, I am sending you." And with that he breathed on them and said, "Receive the Holy Spirit. If you forgive anyone his sins, they are forgiven; if you do not forgive them, they are not forgiven"' (John 20:21). The preacher of, or witness to, the gospel is given here the same watchman role that Ezekiel received. Response to faithful witness leads to salvation, but refusal and rejection retain people's sins and fix them indelibly upon them. The responsibility of the witness is faithful testimony in the power of the Spirit.

This must not be misinterpreted in terms of throwing a message at people's heads without any concern for their welfare or the depths of their response. The responsibility of the witness is a real and deep one, and Ezekiel was warned not to take it lightly, but he could not be held accountable for the ultimate response, and neither can we. God has his people, and by his Spirit through his Word he will bring them in and draw them to the Saviour. Once we take on ourselves the whole responsibility for turning people round, any means of persuasion becomes legitimate, the Lord is turned from being the God who calls for repentance into the beggar crying for entrance and the gospel becomes yet another ideology competing in the market-place.

Ezekiel was now beginning to see more clearly the role he was to play. His vision of God had an end in view, and that end was a message from God to his own contemporaries, which they had no inclination to accept but which they needed to hear. Equipped to withstand their opposition, Ezekiel found to his surprise that accepting God's purpose for himself and his people was finally sweet to his taste. The vision renewed his conviction and experience, and the word imparted content and direction. He could not have managed without either. Nor could he have survived without God's enabling power day by day.

3.
The power of God

The vision of God flung Ezekiel on his face, and the power
of the Spirit of God set him on his feet. Called as he was
to challenge the accepted views of his generation at almost
every point, he was quite incapable of sustaining his
ministry without the power of God. It was the Holy
Spirit who gave him that power.

The receptive power: enabling him to hear

The Spirit came to the prostrate Ezekiel, entered into
him, raised him to his feet and opened his ears to hear
what God was saying (2:2). He was then enabled to
announce with authority: 'This is what the Sovereign
Lord says . . .' (2:4). 1 Corinthians 2:6–16 expounds
this role of the Spirit as the illuminator of God's servants,
revealing to them the truth of God. Without him, the mind
is dull and dark and incapable even of conceiving God's
good purposes for men. With his illumination we may
know the 'thoughts of God' and 'we may understand
what God has freely given us'.

When it comes to the things of God, human intellect
alone is insufficient. Indeed, warped as it is by our sinful
nature, the wisdom of the world can lead to such mon-
strosities as crucifying the Lord of glory in the name of
reason, or seeking to exterminate a whole race. It is Spirit-
given illumination which enables the intellect to function
truly. Unaided human reason degenerates into rationalism,

while illuminated thinking leads to truth. But truth has to be applied to ordinary human living. Ezekiel was enabled by the Spirit to do just that, and the same Spirit is available to us.

This ministry of the Spirit was married closely to a clear word from God with understandable content. We have already seen that this is an essential part of God's dealings with men and women. The Word and the Spirit go together. Paul preached the Word of God, but he did it in the power of the Spirit and not in word only. We cannot afford to separate the Spirit's ministry from the Word, much less set them against each other.

The illuminating power: enabling him to see

Hearing and knowing the truth of God for our day is one thing; seeing where it applies to life and society is quite another. The church of God today is well equipped with the knowledge of the truth of God and his Word, but woefully lacking in seeing where it really applies to daily life and society. So theology has become an intellectual pursuit, more and more divorced from street, factory and office, and the church has become a massive irrelevancy to which no one pays any attention.

The Spirit of God saw to it that Ezekiel would not be faced by this problem. In chapter 8 we read how he took Ezekiel on a guided tour of his own community. While Ezekiel was sitting with the elders of Israel in his own house, 'a figure like that of a man' appeared to him and 'the Spirit lifted me up between earth and heaven and in visions of God took me to Jerusalem'. The actual things that he saw there we shall consider later. For now we should notice that he said to Ezekiel, 'Look' (8:5), and 'Son of man, do you *see* what they are doing . . .? But you will *see* things that are even more detestable' (8:6).

Again, the Spirit directed Ezekiel to enter a private room
in the temple and to '*see* the wicked and detestable things
they are doing here'. 'So I went in and *looked*, and
I *saw*. . .' he says, and once more the Spirit asked him,
'Son of man, have you *seen* . . .?' 'You will *see* them. . .',
'Do you *see* this, son of man?' (8:9—15.)

Many of the sights to which the Spirit of God directed
Ezekiel's attention were commonplace events in the daily
life of Israel. Everyone knew that they happened, but
nobody cared. For Ezekiel to be able to minister to his
people effectively he had to learn to see his society from
God's point of view, and to make that viewpoint his own.
Until we learn to do this, we shall continue to tolerate
the intolerable and to pass over the detestable, and we
shall make no worthwhile impact in our own day and
generation. We need the Spirit's insight.

The depth of insight experienced by Ezekiel is made
clear in chapter 11. There the Spirit led him to the gate
of the house of the Lord, and he saw particular individuals
who were pointed out as leaders of the evil advice being
given to the inhabitants of Jerusalem (11:1,2). In the
vision, Ezekiel seems to have been able to communicate
with these men and address words from the Lord to them,
and while he was speaking one of them dropped down
dead. In times of revival, similar insight into particular
sins of communities and individuals has been given to
God's servants, as God puts his finger on sore spots in
conviction or judgement. The Spirit of God brought the
insight to Ezekiel and gave him the words to say.

The enabling power of his ministry

Not only did the Spirit give Ezekiel insight into the needs
of his people and the particular problems of his day, but
it was he who set him on his feet, sent him out to preach,

communicated the message to him and transported him in visions from one place to another. Chapter 3:22 describes Ezekiel's sense of compulsion as 'the hand of the Lord . . . upon me', which appears to be almost synonymous with the work of the Holy Spirit. In 3:24 the Spirit again raised Ezekiel to his feet, and this time gave him the seemingly strange instructions to go and shut himself inside his house, be bound with ropes and be unable to speak until the Spirit loosed his tongue. Because we so often identify the work of the Spirit with activity, we find it hard to appreciate that he can stop people speaking as much as cause them to speak.

This experience of being seized by the Spirit and carried along by him was by no means an easy or pleasant one. Ezekiel was a son of man, a very ordinary human being, and his emotions were involved. When the Spirit lifted him up and took him away (3:14), he not only went with a conscious sense of the strong hand of the Lord upon him, but also in bitterness and anger. The whole experience left him in a state of overwhelming shock for seven days. We can imagine what our own feelings would be like if we were suddenly taken into the very presence of God and given a world-shattering message for our own people that cut right across everything they believed in and were doing. How could he accept such a commission, and yet did he have a choice to refuse?

Many a servant of God has to a greater or lesser degree felt this ambivalence. On the one hand there is the sense of privilege at being allowed to share the insights of the Spirit and commissioned to pass them on, and on the other an emotional turmoil at the thought of taking up such a high and demanding privilege. Only the compulsion and enabling of the Holy Spirit of God can sustain such people and keep them at their post. Yet they are the people we need in the church today.

The sense of the power of the Spirit in 3:12 was

accompanied by a loud rushing sound, which Ezekiel describes as the wings of the living creatures brushing against each other. Such a sound was heard on the day of Pentecost, where it is described as 'like the blowing of a violent wind [coming] from heaven'. Similar phenomena are often experienced alongside earthquakes and other earthly expressions of might and irresistible power. The sound of the living creatures' wings in the vision of chapter 1:24 was similarly spoken of as 'like the roar of rushing waters'. Indeed, throughout that vision the ministry of the Spirit of God was inextricably entwined with the activities of the living creatures and the movings of the divine chariot. The Spirit directed the wheels of the vehicle and caused the whole to move, stay still or rise above the earth in absolute harmony (1:19–21). So the Spirit of God today orchestrates, indwells and urges on the people of God in achieving his purposes in the world. Just as the life of Jesus perfectly showed the power of a life completely yielded to and directed by the Spirit, so lives that follow his draw all their driving force from that same Spirit. Ezekiel also knew that same compelling urge that kept him moving forward through opposition and suffering as the divine wind filled his sails.

Even more remarkable is the long-sighted view of the ministry of the Spirit revealed to Ezekiel. Even during the long vision of the terrible state of Jerusalem that stretches from chapters 8 to 11, the Lord promises to bring his sinful people back to their land again, free from their 'vile images and detestable idols', and to 'give them an undivided heart and put a new spirit in them; I will remove from them their heart of stone and give them a heart of flesh' (11:18,19). Chapter 36:24–29 goes even further as it identifies this spirit to be put within God's people with God's Spirit. The place of the Spirit of God in the economy of God begins to break through in this remarkable book, and only the Spirit himself can have enabled Ezekiel to see such things.

In the Spirit of God, therefore, we find the empowering force of Ezekiel's ministry. The effect of a vision might easily wear off after a time. The impact of the Word of God might grow stale. But so long as the Spirit of God himself was there, impelling Ezekiel forward, touching on this point and that, stirring him out of his comfortable ruts and pushing him into the arena of public confrontation, God's work would go forward. I have been in ministry long enough to know some of the dangers of professionalism, the weakening of the first thrill at handling the truth of God, and the danger of mechanical reactions replacing living experience. Only the Spirit of God can preserve us from such pitfalls. Only he can revive his church with a new dynamic that will compel the world to listen or, if they will not do so, at least to know that God has been speaking to them.

Ezekiel needed vision, word and Spirit fully to round off his experience and equip him for service. No one aspect of his experience could be taken away without impairing his usefulness. So we need a full-orbed experience of Father, Son and Holy Spirit to keep us evenly balanced, clearly seeing and eagerly proclaiming the message of God. What that involved for Ezekiel and may involve for us, we can now begin to examine.

4.
The times of Ezekiel

Many people do not have too much interest in history, so some readers may be tempted to skip this chapter. Yet when we begin to look into the times of Ezekiel we find so many parallels to our own day, and so many similar problems, that it is only then we can begin to realize how relevant his message is for us. In addition, no one can truly be understood except against the background of his or her environment.

A time of political upheaval

Crises in the Middle East are no modern invention. The Lord settled his people in the most strategic piece of real estate in the whole world. Time and time again it has become the key to political power and therefore the centre of political struggle. Ezekiel's day was no exception.

The superpowers of his time, the sixth century B.C., were Egypt and Babylon, Assyria having been eclipsed by Babylon some years earlier. Egypt was definitely number two, but had been experiencing a time of revived strength under Pharaoh Neco, while Babylon was only growing to her full strength and had little energy left over for foreign adventures. Palestine and the surrounding countries were the satellite states; just as Russia sees Eastern Europe as a buffer against the West, so Babylon saw Palestine and its neighbours as a buffer against Egyptian influence.

Sitting uncomfortably in the middle was the tiny kingdom of Judah. By this time the rest of Israel had been devastated by the Assyrians and resettled by a mixed community. Things were very unsettled at home, too. People lived under the constant threat of war and invasion from one or other of the superpowers, with the other one always angling for influence. Such a time called for clear-sighted strong leadership, but it just was not there. The average age of the last four kings of Judah on their accession was only twenty-two. Two of them only lasted three months before being replaced, one by the Egyptians and the other by the Babylonians. Both of the others lasted eleven years, and both lost their thrones after rebellion against their superpower overlord in Babylon. Zedekiah, the last of all, not only lost the throne, but brought about the destruction of Jerusalem and the total exile of most of the people. When Zedekiah became king, the cream of the community had been transported to Babylon to lessen the possibility of revolt, and Ezekiel had been taken too. So in Ezekiel's lifetime, Jerusalem was led by second-rate little men, with limited views and the stubborn conviction that because Israel was God's people and the temple was still standing in Jerusalem, nothing could ultimately go wrong.

They had some of their own history on their side. Some years before, Jerusalem had been besieged by the Assyrian army which had already destroyed neighbouring Samaria, capital of the northern kingdom of Israel. Like Britain in 1940, the country was threatened with its worst danger for centuries. But under Hezekiah's leadership the city stood firm and the prophet Isaiah promised that the invaders would not be allowed to touch God's own city and its people. Overnight the enemy army had disappeared, leaving the people with an assurance of God's favour and a miracle of his deliverance. So Jerusalem could look back with the confidence that God would never allow anyone to desecrate Jerusalem. But just as Britain in 1984 is a very different country from the Britain of 1940, so Jerusalem was a very different city in Zedekiah's day and her leaders were men of a much inferior calibre. Not all conclusions drawn from history are correct.

What the leaders of Jerusalem in Ezekiel's time could not see was that the whole moral fibre of the nation was gone. For too long they had lived on spiritual capital, diluting it with syncretism and downright unbelief. With no strong convictions on anything, and toleration of most beliefs about everything, there was no real basis for society. This was reflected in the increasing crime, violence and corruption that, as we shall see, permeated society from top to bottom. I find too many parallels for comfort between the Jerusalem of Ezekiel's day and the decline of Western societies in our day. That is why I believe his message has so much to say to us.

With this background in mind, we can go on to see that Ezekiel's message divides into three distinct but related parts, following the introductory section of the vision. The first part, up to chapter 24, gives a picture of almost unrelieved gloom, warnings of inevitable judgement and an analysis of the religious and social reasons why this had to be. The period over which these messages were given lasted until the very day that Jerusalem fell to the Babylonian invader, when the last vain hopes of the people there were shattered on the rocks of reality.

The second part begins with chapter 33, in which Ezekiel was recommissioned. No longer was his message one of judgement and hopelessness, but rather a look forward to an even brighter future than before, with prospects of restoration and renewal by the grace of God. This section takes us to the end of the book.

The third section is sandwiched in the middle, when the prophet addressed the sins and problems of the surrounding societies and nations, showing that the

Sovereign Lord of the universe has no favourites and
that the moral and spiritual rules that govern the world
are of universal application. This section will not concern
us very much in this book, but we do need to know that
it is there.

No one wants to face a message of doom and gloom,
and our own generation has been nourished on our right
to enjoy life and happiness, with everything offered to
us on a plate. Anyone who injects a note of reality tends
to be dismissed as a wet blanket or caricatured as a crank.
Ezekiel had no choice about what he had to proclaim,
and he certainly was not very popular, until eventually
Jerusalem did fall and his words were proved right.
Unfortunately, by then it was too late to produce change
and Ezekiel was only left with the doubtful privilege of
being able to say, 'I told you so.'

In the same way, we live in a society that does not
want to face the realities of the spiritual and moral
situation confronting us, but we cannot as Christians hide
our heads in the sand and refuse to face some of the same
factors that call out for the judgement of God, simply
because to do so would make us unpopular. We do still
have time to say and do something about our situation,
and as watchmen for our own society we have a responsibility to do so. We must therefore tackle the first section
of Ezekiel's book with a desire for the Spirit to speak
to us about things as they really are, enabling us to know
what we should do.

The threatening cloud

5.
Sounding the alarm

Chapters 4–7 of Ezekiel give us little to encourage us. His ministry began with a series of visual demonstrations that did nothing to convince his contemporaries of his sanity. He certainly made an impact and no one could doubt afterwards that he was talking about a coming judgement. Perhaps he had to do it that way to break through the massive wall of apathy and indifference that surrounded the people. Ordinary methods no longer spoke to them.

Chapter 4 describes how he played soldiers in the mud, building up a model of Jerusalem under siege. Then he was told to demonstrate the uncomfortable effects of incarceration within a surrounded city. For days on end he lay on one side or the other, eating famine fare. At first he was told to cook it on human excrement, as people did actually have to do during the siege, but then as a concession he was allowed to use the more frequently burnt fuel of cow manure. Before we turn away in disgust, we should remember that this is the kind of fuel some people in our modern world in their poverty still have to use.

When Ezekiel obeyed the instructions given him in chapter 5, some people must really have thought he had gone out of his head. First he shaved both his head and his beard, and then he weighed the hair and divided it into three parts. One third he burnt with fire in his model city, the second third he hacked to pieces with a sword, and the last part he threw up into the air when the wind

was blowing. Even that was not the finish. He had to
save a few strands of hair and tuck them into the folds
of his clothes, and then take even some of those and
burn them. By that time there was little left, and that,
of course, was God's message to the people. They had
reached a stage when the fire, sword and plague of God's
judgement was the only alternative to a real repentance.
They had reached the point of no return. Complacency
no longer would do. They either had to wake up or die.

Chapter 6 expresses in plain language what Ezekiel's
strange antics had so dramatically illustrated. The Lord's
people, who at one time had honoured and walked with
him, had gone so far in the opposite direction that there
was only one way they could be woken up to the fact
that God was not a creation of their own imagination,
but a real living person who holds men morally accountable. That was by his calling them to account in judgement. Only after that would they sit up and take notice
that 'I am the Lord'.

There comes a time in some societies when God has
become so remote that his reality is totally discounted.
We live in such societies in the West today. The problem
does not lie in the fact that men and women reject our
belief in God, but rather that they treat it as a belief and
nothing more. They do not for a moment imagine that
there is a God who really exists and who will call them
to account. 'You are welcome to hold your beliefs,' they
say, 'if by pretending that God exists you get some help
with your weaknesses or see some meaning in life, but
please do not ask anyone else to take seriously this
invention of your imaginations and projection of your
infirmities.' Is there anything that can wake such a
generation to the terrible situation in which they place
themselves by writing off their Creator and dismissing
him who *is* as dead? Perhaps Ezekiel's drama was
necessary.

Chapter 7 has an even more modern ring to it. Ezekiel's message was that 'The end! The end has come . . .' (7:2). A modern Westerner immediately has in his mind's eye the picture of a man walking down the street with a sandwich-board on his back or a banner in his hand bearing the words: 'Prepare to meet thy God.' Ezekiel would have been described in the press today as a 'doom and gloom merchant', and that is to place yourself in the category of a reject. But Ezekiel was not put off. 'Disaster! An unheard-of disaster is coming. The end has come! The end has come! It has roused itself against you. It has come! Doom has come upon you — you who dwell in the land. The time has come, the day is near; there is panic, not joy, upon the mountains' (7:5—7).

There comes a time when a man does have to meet his God, and Ezekiel lived in such a time. He had good cause, too, for warning of the calamity that was coming. He could see the army of Babylon, the superpower, exercising near the refugee camps, as it assembled for the invasion of Israel. Ezekiel was not talking through his hat under a clear sky. He had a basis for calling his people to repentance. And we have just as much, if not more. He knew nothing of atomic or hydrogen bombs, germ warfare or weapons of mass destruction. He had never heard of S20s pointed at Jerusalem and Pershing and Cruise missiles facing the other way. He simply knew that power politics were explosive, and that moral and religious factors played a bigger part in determining the outcome of human struggles than any of his contemporaries were prepared to admit. He could see that the moral fibre of his nation was gone, so that when the invasion did come 'every hand will go limp, and every knee will become as weak as water' (7:17); 'When terror comes, they will seek peace, but there will be none' (7:25). People would awake to reality, but too late, and war and invasion would leave little opportunity to get things right and build moral fences. The end of this chapter pictured the people turning frantically to prophets, priests and elders, only to find that at that stage they had nothing to offer. Even 'the King will mourn, the prince will be clothed with despair, and the hands of the people of the land will tremble' (7:27). The time to build the moral fibre of a nation is before the crisis comes and Ezekiel was seeking to awake his people to the need for this. But his message fell on deaf ears.

One of the problems about sounding the spiritual alarm is that until disaster strikes people want to continue in their state of comfortable illusion, reckoning that the *status quo* may last for ever. Anyone who injects a slice of reality at that point is bound to sound a jarring note and is likely to be answered, 'It has not happened yet,' with the unspoken assumption that it never will. No doubt Ezekiel would have been glad to see his loved Jerusalem spared, but God had awakened him to indications of collapse that he could not ignore, so, as a responsible watchman, he had to sound the alarm. We also might reckon that our generation may pass without a Third World War or the use of atomic weapons. But anyone looking out on the power politics of our day, seeing the stockpiling of these weapons and knowing the human heart in the least degree, must realize that the possibilities of conflict are very high indeed.

In such a context, the very worst danger lies in the moral and spiritual collapse of a people and that, I believe, is where our danger lies today. We cannot necessarily prevent emergencies arising, but we can see to it that, by the grace of God, people are ready to meet them as far as possible. Therefore we need to study Ezekiel's analysis of his own day and generation and see if his diagnosis has any relevance to ours.

6.
Syncretism and false religion

The decline of any society begins with the erosion of its basis for existence, for a culture is held together by the cement of common convictions. In most Western societies, the common belief for centuries centred around some form of Christianity, but no one can dispute that in the last hundred years real commitment to the truth of the gospel has declined steadily. While the shell may still be there, and some vague attachment is sometimes expressed, real conviction is rare. But man is fundamentally a believer and cannot live in an ideological vacuum. So when the truth is doubted, then the false flourishes. If man does not have a religion of his own, he will either create one or take a copy. The usual tendency is for people to part from what used to be accepted and be drawn to the new ideas being marketed, for the old religion has become a part of an old establishment and therefore few people will bother to stop and ask whether in fact the new is better than the old. They simply want something in which to believe and the new doctrines have an inviting freshness about them.

We find this process taking place in Judah in Ezekiel's day. After underlining the necessity of judgement, the Spirit of God directs our attention in chapter 8 to Judah's decline in her allegiance to the Lord. Ezekiel was sitting with some of the elders in Babylon when the Spirit transported him to Jerusalem. His guide was the man who sat on the throne in the vision, and he took Ezekiel by the Spirit to the north gate of the inner court of the temple.

41

Ezekiel found two contradictory scenes before him: one
is described as 'the glory of the God of Israel, as in the
vision I had seen on the plain'. The other was 'the idol
that provokes to jealousy' (8:3—5).

There, in the very nerve-centre of the worship of God,
stood the symbol of a rival belief, a constant irritation
to the worshipper who knew that there was only one living
God, who is the Lord. What was so offensive was that this
idol was set up in the very centre of the temple itself,
not in some rival conventicle across the road. Obviously
people had become so used to it that it no longer drew
any comment. Familiarity breeds not only contempt but
toleration. No doubt to many this was a symbol of their
broad-mindedness, a welcome expansion of belief to
embrace the ideas of surrounding nations. God describes
it as an 'idol that provokes to jealousy' (8:3).

The real question that so many people were avoiding
was the distinction between truth and error. Most of them
felt that their belief in the Lord was simply the way they
had been brought up. It was probably a good way, but
other peoples had other beliefs and tolerance required
that those beliefs be accepted as equally valid. Who were
they to tell the other person he was wrong? That surely
was bigotry. Also, some of those foreign nations seemed
to be remarkably successful politically and economically,
so perhaps there was more to their religions than narrow-
thinking conservatives were prepared to admit. There
was a big wide world outside the confines of Israel, and
while people in David's time (400 years before) could
be forgiven for thinking that Israel was the centre of
the universe, the modern generation knew better and
was therefore more open to other ideas. Anyone who
persisted in retaining the exclusiveness of the Lord as
the God of Israel and Creator of the world was out of
step with the times, by definition obscurantist and con-
veniently dismissed under some such heading as

'fundamentalist'. The fact that this reasoning begged the whole question of truth and error did not seem to enter their thinking. Everyone took it for granted that religion was a matter of belief, and belief is a matter of opinion, not a question of right or wrong, black or white. Therefore in issues of religion, everything had to be a shade of grey and anyone who resisted such thinking must be reactionary.

These are the very attitudes that we face today. Definite convictions concerning God, life, death, eternity, heaven and hell are frowned upon as necessarily arrogant and opinionated. We have to face these questions squarely and take into account far-reaching implications. For example, what about the disastrous effects in human history of religious movements so convinced of the truth of their viewpoint that they have persecuted those with other ideas and thus caused untold human misery? Our own day is not without examples of religious intolerance in more than one religion. These bad examples, also found in modern Christian circles, drive people away from any exclusive claim for any one religion or branch of a religion. Yet, at the same time, we cannot ignore the fact that when the Spirit of God took Ezekiel on a conducted tour of Judah's various religious manifestations, described most of them as 'detestable' things — hardly the language of tolerance (8:6, 9, 10).

We must therefore consider whether an exclusive form of belief has any validity, and if so, whether it necessarily leads to intolerance, bigotry and persecution. In other disciplines an attitude of exclusiveness is very common, yet rarely leads to violence or intolerance. No one ever suggests that two plus two equals anything but four! We are fairly sure that that statement accords with reality and therefore is true. We do not suggest that we should be tolerant of those who believe that two plus two equals three and a half, because really their opinion on these

matters has to be respected as much as ours. But in another
sense we are tolerant towards such people, because we are
sure their belief is wrong, however sincere, and in the
long run they are the ones who will lose out. We believe
that for their own sakes we should try to convince them
of the mistake they are making, but if they persist in
their belief they pose no threat to us mathematically
speaking.

Why do we abandon this kind of thinking when it
comes to questions of ultimate reality? Why should
allegiance to revealed truth be considered the height of
intolerance? Why must it be affirmed that all roads lead
to God, when we do not accept that all sums lead to
mathematical accuracy? Quite clearly the Lord wanted
Ezekiel to see things differently. Although Judah had
abandoned the exclusiveness of her allegiance to the Lord,
the Spirit of God had not changed his mind on the subject.
God had only condemnation for the presence of rival
systems of worship in his sanctuary. Therefore to abandon
the concepts of truth and error because of the intolerance
of ᵗ ᵐe systems associated with Christianity is an over-
rea ᵗ ᵒn.

ᵗct exclusiveness in belief should never lead to
int ᵗ ᵃance in attitude if that belief corresponds to reality
Of all people Christians should be the most tolerant ar
yet the most firm in their convictions. If what they believe
is really the truth of the living God, revealed by him to
men and not thought up by men about him, they cannot
afford to dilute that truth. On the other hand, they, of all
people, should feel the least threatened by other ideas.
If what they believe is indeed the truth, then ultimately
it will be shown to be such. They do not therefore need
to throw their weight about in self-defence. Their Lord
was the living embodiment of all truth and is called the
Truth, yet when rejected and assaulted and decried he
calmly committed himself to the Sovereign Lord. When

his enemies had done their worst, that confidence was completely justified in his resurrection from the dead. You cannot kill truth.

There is, in fact, some evidence that Christians are more tolerant than most. Many nations with a Christian history impose no restrictions on the entry of foreign nationals who desire to propagate another religion within their borders. They may limit them for other reasons, but rarely for religious ones. On the other hand, many nations that owe allegiance to other religions place severe restrictions on Christians who wish to propagate their faith, arguing that 'freedom of religion' within the United Nations charter only means freedom to practise the religion you already have, and not freedom to hear what others believe or to change your mind.

Therefore for a Christian to have a firm conviction concerning truth and error is not necessarily a prelude to intolerance and bigotry. Indeed, the deeper his commitment to truth, the deeper his confidence that, like the Servant in Isaiah, he has no need to lift up his voice and shout in the street when presenting that truth to others (Isaiah 42:2).

At the same time, none should be as firm in his hold upon truth as the Christian. The sad fact in Judah was that the very people who should have been standing most strongly for the truth of God were openly welcoming other, contradictory beliefs into the heart of their own religion. That image at the north gate of the inner court presented an open affront to the Lord and the truth about him. Such action God described as 'utterly detestable': such worship was calculated to drive the Lord far from his sanctuary, not draw him to his people.

Is it really any different when leaders of the Church of England openly take part in an inter-faith service in Westminster Abbey? What is being said by such services in such a key place of worship is that there is really no vital

difference between the religions of the world and in the
end we will all arrive at the same destination. But the
plain fact is that not all religions are even aiming at the
same destination. Their concepts of what awaits man
beyond this life are totally different and their concepts
of 'God' vary enormously. In fact, many have no real
idea of God as an existent being at all. To them God is
simply the sum total of existence and their greatest
hope is to be absorbed into the whole, to lose their
individuality and therefore their pain and suffering. They
are, of course, entitled to hold those beliefs. But for
Christian leaders to pretend that when they join in worship
with such friends they are addressing one and the same
God is to make nonsense of revelation and reduce God's
message to a philosophy. Mathematicians might smile in
sympathy at those who insisted on proclaiming that two
plus two equals three and a half, but they would never
join in a project with them on anything that required
mathematical accuracy. Designing an aeroplane with
such sincere believers would be a programme for disaster,
not tolerance.

The image of jealousy that Ezekiel was shown at the
entrance of the temple represented a clear departure
from the original faith of Israel and offered an ins
to the one true God, Lord and Creator of heaven an
earth, seen clearly in the vision of chapter 1. But worse
was to follow. At the guide's invitation Ezekiel dug into
a wall at the entrance to the court, and a door stood
revealed there. He was told to go inside and take a look
at what was going on. The sight that met his eyes sickened
him. 'I saw portrayed all over the walls all kinds of crawl-
ing things and detestable animals and all the idols of the
house of Israel' (8:7—10). Seventy of the elders of Israel
stood in front of these pictures with censers in their hands,
each offering worship to his own idol. Hidden from sight
in the recesses of the temple courts, the leaders of God's

people were indulging in the real worship of their hearts. Outwardly they maintained the rituals of the temple, but in reality they had long ago abandoned any real faith in the God of Israel. Their attitude can be summed up in the words of 8:12: 'The Lord does not see us; the Lord has forsaken the land.' To them God was the absentee God. Much more real were the ideas and fancies of the modern generation.

The deepest tragedy of this picture was that these men were supposed to be the guardians of their faith and the exponents of the truth. They lacked the basic integrity and honesty that should have compelled them to leave these positions and openly align themselves with the ungodly. We see the same symptoms in the church of God today. Men who have long since abandoned any belief in the reality of Jesus Christ, his virgin birth, his real resurrection and ascension and the reality of heaven and hell continue to hold office in churches and seminaries. In our day they do not always have the decency to carry on their strange worship in the dark, as Israel's elders did, but openly parade their unbelief and publicly advocate departure from Christian truth, in morals as well as religion, in the name of progress. The one subject on which they are united is opposition to the teaching of the Bible as the Word of God, and the proclaiming of Jesus Christ as mankind's one and only Saviour. Ezekiel chapter 8 warns us that the living God is fully aware of such activities and, far from seeing them as evidence of the up-to-date nature of the Christianity they represent, regards them as cause for judgement on apostasy. The rot that was destroying Israel's society in those days began at this very point.

Ezekiel was taken still further. As he came to the north gate of the house of the Lord he saw women sitting mourning for Tammuz (8:14, 15). Tammuz was a Babylonian deity, the god of vegetation, who was thought to die and rise again in the cycle of the seasons. So these women were doing exactly what their neighbours did, except that they happened also to believe in the Lord. Tolerance for man's imaginings alongside God's revealed truth leads unerringly to assimilation of religion with the surrounding culture. Why be different from people who surround you if there is no need to be? Why stick out like a sore thumb if you can melt into the scenery? When everyone knew what the religious leaders were doing and their lack of commitment to the truth of God, why should these women not join their neighbours in their celebrations? When in Babylon, do as Babylon does.

Pressure to conform to surrounding customs and beliefs is always strong, and additional pressure comes on Christians today in their desire to make the gospel relevant to contemporary society. But we must be aware of the dangers involved in this process. In many Western lands the church has tried so hard to be relevant that it has ceased to be different. Unaware of the subtle slide into conformity, many Christians have been totally swallowed up by the surrounding materialism and the only difference between their lives and those of their neighbours is in what they do for an hour or so on Sunday.

No wonder then that the final scene in chapter 8 shows twenty-five elders of Jerusalem 'with their backs towards the temple of the Lord and their face towards the east', who 'were bowing down to the sun in the east' (8:16). This chapter repeats the old fable of the camel and the tent. The traveller in the story camped in the desert with his camel outside. Soon the camel was asking to come in out of the cold, promising only to intrude his neck, but before long the camel had taken over and the man was out in the cold. What began in tolerance ended in a take-over. Truth reduced to an opinion carried no more weight than any other view. So the elders turned their backs on the temple and gave their attention and adoration to the

7.
Preachers with nothing to say

A community is as strong as its leadership. A church is as strong as its ministry. The truth of God is always the same, but the application of that truth to each generation is always different. Luther's generation needed to hear of justification by faith; Wesley's and Whitefield's needed to know how to find assurance. Some churches need encouragement and the calm voice of peaceful assurance, while others must hear the trumpet-call of judgement and the challenge to repentance. Those who can see through to the need of their own generation are its indispensable prophets. Their ministry must be sensitive. They must be alert to the need of the hour and to the message God has for that hour. Such sensitivity is not acquired in ten minutes on a Saturday night because a sermon must be preached next day. Yet preachers must preach and prophets must prophesy; that is their calling and ministry. The tragedy occurs when the message of the preacher or prophet is nothing more than the banal utterance of a religious professional. Israel in Ezekiel's day was full of religious professionals, not in the sense that they knew their job, but in the sense that they only did it for a living and not because of the impelling force of God's Spirit.

This kind of professionalism in the ministry destroys a people. When the standard of preaching goes down, so does the quality of Christian faith and life. Our own generation is an outstanding example of this truth, so much so that many people wish to have done with

preaching and the placing of a man 'six feet above contra-
diction'. We are sometimes told that 'This congregation
will not listen for more than ten minutes, so please do
not go beyond that.' When that happens there is something seriously wrong. Ezekiel's day did not lack for preaching that claimed to be inspired. The number of so-called
prophets was legion. But their impact on society for good
was negligible and indeed counter-productive. Chapter 13
of Ezekiel's book makes clear that there is a very real
connection between a disintegrating society and a dis-
credited pulpit.

Before examining the critique of the prophets that
Ezekiel introduced by saying, 'The word of the Lord came
to me . . .', it is necessary to explain the role of these
prophets in Israel's society. The priests in the temple
were to instruct the people in the truths of the law of
God, to interpret the law for the people and to give rulings
about it. The prophets, on the other hand, delivered to
God's people the messages they had received from him
and called them to respond to him. They were the vision-
aries of the people of God, imp: rection to the life
of the nation, presenting challenges for response and
questioning the clichés. Their role was not so much to
foretell the future as to 'forth-tell' the Word of God to
the present.

As I see it, that is exactly the role that the preaching
ministry should fulfil in the church of God today. The
problem in Ezekiel's day, and sometimes in ours, too, was
that the rich, stimulating, cathartic, challenge of the Word
of God, carefully applied by men with a vision, had been
watered down to little more than the milk of human kind-
ness flavoured by a desire to please. What had gone wrong?

Their preaching never rose higher than their own minds

The preaching of the prophets was limited to the resources of their own human thinking. Ezekiel condemned them because they 'prophesy out of their own imagination . . . follow their own spirit and have seen nothing . . . Their visions are false and their divinations a lie . . . The Lord has not sent them' (13:2–6). Quite clearly these prophets had received nothing from God for his people. They were supposed to speak, so they spoke, but their words were only humanistic reasoning. The congregation never felt that God had been speaking to them, and left the place as unmoved by God as they entered it. There was nothing in the preaching that they could not get from their local newspaper — in fact some of their politicians had more to say and said it better. For when the truth of God is not proclaimed, the product of the human imagination turns out to be not only uninspiring, but often a lie. And when the preacher is not sent by God, he has nothing to say from God. We who are preachers need constantly to examine ourselves before scriptures like this, for I meet with Christians from many countries who, time and time again, say to me, 'We get nothing from the sermons in our church.' 'We never get any consecutive teaching.' 'We are not made to feel that the Bible is applicable to today.' 'We are hungry and we are not fed.' Where such feelings are expressed, something must be wrong.

The practice of exposition of Scripture has largely died out in the pulpits of our churches. Certainly the *idea* of exposition is very much in vogue, but what passes for exposition so often turns out to be anything but that, varying from clear imposition upon the text of Scripture to 'blessed thoughts' that have some vague relation to an overall passage. One clear test is whether it is possible to sit through a message with the Bible shut, or even

without a Bible at all. If that is the case, little or no exposition is taking place. Yet the role of the modern preacher/
prophet is to take that Word of God and apply its pene-
trating analysis and challenge to the daily life of the people
of God. Some have so given up hope of hearing such a
ministry that they rely almost entirely on the extempore
prophecy of those who feel they have the gift directly
from God. In fact, some would even decry the preaching
of the Word of God as being the application of the letter
that kills. They claim primacy for the spoken utterance
of the prophet. Yet prophecies of this kind can also come
from the mind of the prophet and no higher, just as really
as preaching can come from the mind of the preacher and
no more. This is quite apart from the fact that the distinction made between the letter and the spirit in 2 Corinthians 3 was never meant to be used to drive a wedge
between the Word of God written and the Word preached
or spoken.

Their preaching deceived their hearers by its use of language

The prophets used the right language to gain a hearing and
the people were deceived into thinking they meant what
they said. Although the Lord had not spoken to them or
sent them, they could still attach the formula 'The Lord
declares' to their utterance (13:6). They even expected
their words to be fulfilled when they talked of future
deliverance and blessing, based on what they conceived to
be the promises of God. To gain a hearing from believers,
a certain language may need to be used, but when that
phraseology degenerates into cliché without meaning,
the end result is worse than useless. Expectations are
raised that have no hope of fulfilment. H. L. Ellison in
his commentary says, 'It is not the unsound or worldly

teacher or preacher who is the real danger to the church, but the man who allows himself so to be dominated by his own deepest desires that he is preaching them, although convinced himself that it is the Word of God that he is preaching.'[1] This is a very subtle and dangerous problem. I once heard someone describe it as 'baptizing our own desires'.

As great a danger today are those who proclaim 'another gospel', but clothe their message in the language of orthodoxy. Though using words that for centuries have conveyed the truth of God, they use them with a totally different meaning. They talk of the resurrection, while disbelieving in the historical resurrection of Jesus Christ and meaning simply the idea of dying to an old form of living and rising to a new one. The nature religions of old had this concept, and without the historical resurrection of Jesus Christ it remains a concept without power. It is only as we identify with a death and resurrection that took place in time, space and history, that there is any power in the new life in Christ, for then he is the living Lord.

We must therefore recognize that the use of orthodox religious language or evangelical terminology is no guarantee of a message from God. There can be talk of the Lord without a knowledge of the Lord. There can even be sincere belief in the nature of the preaching and an expectation that God will honour it. The religious professional may be unaware of the emptiness of his message and this fact calls for careful discernment on the part of God's people and prayer for those who minister. Evangelical preachers are not immune from such problems, for when a message comes purely from the mind of the preacher and is not drawn from the content and meaning of the Word of God, simply attaching a text to it does nothing to validate its credentials. There is a dangerous borderline between the true and the false, between exaggerated claims for human ideas and the genuine authority of the Word of God. There is a narrow difference between views expressed dogmatically and the Word of God proclaimed in the power of the Spirit. Both come with conviction, one from a human source, the other from a divine one.

Their preaching had no practical or useful effect

Plenty of hot air resulted in no heart change: conduct remained the same. Eloquence had no effect on execution. Ezekiel described the prophets as like foxes or jackals among the ruins (13:4). They had failed to go up 'to the breaks in the wall to repair it for the house of Israel so that it will stand firm in the battle on the day of the Lord'. The language is that of a city under siege, a condition with which Jerusalem was only too familiar. Any city under siege depended upon the strength of its walls to survive, and the walls were only as strong as their weakest point. The responsibility of the leaders of society was to see that the walls were kept intact and the weakest points reinforced. But the prophets, far from building up the weak points, allowed the defensive perimeter to disintegrate. A fox or a jackal made no contribution to the defence. They either undermined the walls further or, in their total ignorance of the dangers, cheerfully knocked more pieces off them. Walther Eichrodt suggests that the fox is in fact at home in ruins. So the prophets not only did not view Israel's inward and outward downfall as a calamity, but 'They feel perfectly at ease in this disaster, they enjoy it and even make themselves at home in it and exploit it!'[2]

Whatever the precise picture conveyed by the foxes or jackals, the meaning generally is clear. When a society is morally wanting, there are gaping holes in its fabric —

dangerous holes that can lead to its eventual collapse. Holes in the moral and spiritual defences of a nation cannot be plugged by missiles and tanks. The problem goes much too deep for that. Preachers of the Word of God are called to draw attention to the holes and to declare God's message in such a way that the people are restored. But Israel's prophets were powerless to make any impact on their society. For all their preaching, lives were not changed, society continued to disintegrate and moral decay was not arrested.

One of the problems of preaching in the present day also is its seeming powerlessness to change society. Britain in particular has seen a vast influx of evangelical preachers into the ministry in the last thirty years, and yet the decline in the spiritual state of the country has continued. The fact that the vast majority of the population is not listening may partly account for that. Bright spots shine out here and there, but overall the Christian church is treated as a vast irrelevancy, her ministry portrayed in the media as spineless weaklings and her pronouncements viewed as a voice from the past. Must not we who are preachers ask ourselves what ꞏ ꞏ ꞏ ꞏing? As a person who has to travel widely, I have ꞏ the opportunity of visiting churches as a member of the congregation. Rarely, so rarely have I had to open my Bible at all. Is there any connection between these experiences and our inability to influence the state of our society? The gaps in the spiritual defences of the West are appalling and growing year by year, but where are the builders of the wall?

Their message offered cheap grace and a false peace

The prophets in Ezekiel's time were saying, 'Peace', when there was no peace (13:10). They assured people that all

was well, when things were far from well. They preached
a God of love who would never presume to judge his own
people. The very presence of the temple among them
brought a solid reassurance that they would never be
moved. They exhorted people to trust in God for his
deliverance, but repentance had no place in their
vocabulary.

The temptation in any time of decline, when people
do not respond to the Word of God, is to water down
the message to the level where they are prepared to listen.
That level inevitably reaches the point where no one
must be disturbed. To suggest that there is something
wrong with them is to turn them off, so 'accentuate the
positive and eliminate the negative'. Tell the people there
is peace with God to be found through his love, but do
not suggest that first of all they must abandon their own
wilful warfare against him. Encourage people to decide
for Christ, but keep quiet about repentance.

Ezekiel stated that preaching of this kind leads people
astray. There is no peace with God without repentance.
There is no salvation in Christ without abandoning our
sinful rebellion against God and our wilful choosing of
our own way. Yet the note of challenge on sin and judgement is the lost chord of modern evangelism and preaching. One of the most distressing features of this fact is
that many sincere and dedicated people cannot see it.
Campaigns proliferate, and nowhere so frequently as in
Singapore, where I live. People are urged to come to
Christ and hundreds of 'decisions' are made and rejoiced
over. But time and time again repentance is not men-
tioned, and in some cases even the cross is omitted. Yet
to raise a question mark over such evangelism is not
popular and brings the invariable answer that 'so many'
people made decisions, as though the sheer fact of deciding
something validates the content of the gospel preached.
I have come to the reluctant conclusion that crying peace

where there is no peace is another ancient heresy that is very much alive. No wonder that decisions made on this basis lead to little impact upon society and a lowering of the standards of discipleship. Growth through dilution is worse than no growth at all, for in the long run it saps the energy of the church.

Paul warned Timothy of the time to come, when 'men will not put up with sound doctrine. Instead, to suit their own desires, they will gather around them a great number of teachers to say what their itching ears want to hear. They will turn their ears away from the truth and turn aside to myths' (2 Timothy 4:3). At such a time, the temptation is to dilute the message of the gospel to the level of mediocre acceptability. But the charge Paul gave to Timothy was rather to 'keep your head in all situations, endure hardship, do the work of an evangelist, discharge all the duties of your ministry'. We are not called to be hard-hearted or to hurl bitter denunciations on unreceptive populations, but neither must we lower the standards of the truth of the gospel and pretend there is peace where there is none.

Their preaching simply endorsed the latest world-view

Ezekiel pictures the preaching of these prophets as a whitewash, a cosmetic covering for a totally inadequate proposition. The holes in the wall were being mended with flimsy partitions, plywood sheets or cardboard cartons hastily erected to plug the gap. The building was done by the people; the prophets had failed to provide anything. But when the people had done their best to put something in the yawning holes in the defences, along came the prophets and whitewashed them. This graphic illustration portrays exactly the bankruptcy of ideas within

the church of God. There was a time in history when
Christians were the creative thinkers and the world
followed at a respectful distance. However, for many
years now the world has ceased to look to the church
for anything in the way of a creative contribution to
the desperate needs of the present age. Rather,
rationalistic humanism has been providing its own flimsy
answers and the church has come along, usually ten years
later, to cover the latest opinion with the whitewash
of its endorsement. Richard Lovelace, in his historical
analysis of the *Dynamics of Spiritual Life*, illustrates
the trend from the realm of psychiatry. He writes,
'During the late nineteenth century, while the church's
understanding of the unconscious motivation behind
surface actions was vanishing, Sigmund Freud re-
discovered this factor and recast it in an elaborate and
profound secular mythology.'[3] The process then developed
in reverse. 'One of the consequences of this remarkable
shift is that in the twentieth century pastors have often
been reduced to the status of legalistic moralists, while
the deeper aspects of the cure of souls are generally
relegated to psychotherapy, even among Evangelical
Christians.' Now the bookshops are flooded with
Christian writers on all kinds of counselling, developing
to Christian use the insights of the secular psychologists
and psychiatrists.

I am not suggesting that Christians have nothing to
learn from the study of disciplines generally considered
secular. All that is really true has its origin in the Lord,
for he created the world to work in the way that it does.
The real tragedy is that in the past hundred years Christians have retreated from creative thinking, left the world
to do it and then endorsed the latest world-view, more
often than not uncritically.

Another illustration of this is in the more extreme
forms of the feminist movement. Jesus Christ was the

great liberator of women, but his followers stopped the process somewhere along the way. The secularist world took it up with a vengeance — literally in a vengeful way sometimes, and now some theologians not only endorse every aspect of the whole movement, but take it even further than the secularists.

When Christians cease to do their own creative thinking, they are condemned to follow other people's and lack the discernment to know where to stop. Whitewash covers the whole wall. Who looks to the preacher these days for stimulating and creative thinking on any of the thousand and one pressing problems of our age? And, even more serious, where is the prophetic voice that applies the deep truths of Scripture to the needs of men? Who is prepared to state unequivocally that the real problem with man is his sin, deep-dyed and corrupting everything he does, and that the only answer to that is Jesus Christ?

Ezekiel called people back to the root cause of their distress, their relationship with their God. He was not afraid to repeat old remedies. The disintegration of their society and its imminent judgement had its source in their departure from trust in and obedience to the Lord. The heart had gone out of their society, so there was nothing left to hold it together. What was more, they were not just dealing with an ideology round which to centre their community, but with the living God who rules in the kingdoms of men and who holds people morally accountable. Ezekiel had experienced the awe of seeing the throne of God and the reality of his presence. He therefore spoke with feeling, conviction and power. He could not keep quiet. He had to challenge the *status quo*, even if it meant being a lone voice in a mass of preachers, all of whom were pouring soothing syrup into people who wanted to hear nothing else. I do not believe that the average Western person is looking for soothing syrup. That is why he abandoned church-going many years ago. But do we have the courage to challenge our generation with the living God, and can we respond to the challenge to creative thinking that we have so often left to others?

Whitewash is no defence against the hailstones of God's judgement (13:10–12), and when the wall eventually collapses the people will turn to the prophets of peace with the accusing question: 'Where is the whitewash you covered it with?' God himself declares that he will tear down the wall, that he will hurl his wrath against the wall and against those who covered it with whitewash, and will say to the people, 'The wall is gone and so are those who whitewashed it' (13:13–16). Preachers who simply echo the latest world-view, in their desire to be contemporary, are held responsible for the inevitable result of building defences that cannot stand. It is those who are prepared to challenge society with the Word of God and the call to repentance that are the true friends of the people, however unpopular they may be at the time.

The ultimate result of inadequate preaching

The rest of chapter 13 indicates only too well the effect of poor preaching upon a community. Verses 17–23 paint a picture of all kinds of spiritism, necromancy and superstition that apparently flourished in Jerusalem. Those who fostered this movement were described as 'lying to my people' and those who followed them as 'listening to lies', with the result that the whole moral order was turned upside down (13:19). When truth is at a discount, people will believe anything. So Western society is riddled with all kinds of occult practice. Satanism, the restoration of paganism and fortune-telling, horoscopes and so on. When evil flourishes and truth has lost her voice, inevitably those who want to live a righteous life begin to feel that the situation is hopeless, and the wicked seize the opportunity to do anything they please and legitimize it (13:22).

This scripture is so absolutely up to date today. The forces of evil are militant. Preaching seems to be powerless and when it is heard it often endorses all that is going on. The judgement of God, on the other hand, is that a society in this state is ripe for catastrophe, hollow at its very core. But the people he first calls to account are the preachers. No one seemed to be able to see this in Ezekiel's day. A minority of one, no doubt ostracized by his fellow prophets and labelled obscurantist, intolerant, fundamentalist and out-of-date, he must have been tempted to abandon his crusade and fall into line. Fortunately he did not do so, and ultimately he was proved right. This whole passage challenges me as a preacher to examine my own message and call and to go back to the Lord for his word for a disintegrating society. If we fail, what hope is there of anyone else raising their voice for the living God? Maybe we have to be a minority, and an unpopular one, but the voice has to be heard. The sad thing is that when Ezekiel was proved to be right and God's judgement came, it was already too late.

Footnotes
1. H. L. Ellison, *Ezekiel: The Man and His Message*, Paternoster Press, 1967, p. 5.
2. Walther Eichrodt, *Ezekiel* SCM Press, 1970, p. 163.
3. Richard Lovelace, *Dynamics of Spiritual Life*, IVP USA, 1979, p. 88.

8.
Breach of promise

Grace sparkles like a diamond in Ezekiel's chapter 16. Set against the jet black of Israel's degradation and disobedience, the jewel of God's undeserved mercy shines all the more brightly. Hebrew thinking painted pictures, rather than reasoning in a straight line, and the picture coloured on the canvas of this chapter expresses vividly what grace is all about. It begins with the dark background as the word of the Lord came to Ezekiel once more: 'Son of man, confront Jerusalem with her detestable practices and say . . .' (16:2). Departure from the true and living God stands blacker than ebony in contrast to the beauty of God's free unmerited love. So Ezekiel moves swiftly on to portray the miracle of grace.

The origin of Israel and of man by nature

Nothing in man's history leaves him anything to boast about. 'Your ancestry and birth were in the land of the Canaanites; your father was an Amorite and your mother a Hittite' (16:3). These words must have grated harshly on the ears of a nation that so prided itself on its racial purity. Israel was derived from common human stock. Religious people often need reminding of this fact. Familiarity with worship and spiritual things can breed a false exclusiveness and a pretension to uniqueness. We all need reminding, as Paul wrote to the Ephesian Christians, that 'All of us . . . lived among them [transgressions and sins] at one time, gratifying the cravings of our sinful nature and following its desires and thoughts. Like the rest, we were by nature objects of wrath' (Ephesians 2:3).

'On the day you were born your cord was not cut,' the Lord continues to remind them, 'nor were you washed with water to make you clean, nor were you rubbed with salt or wrapped in cloth. No one looked on you with pity or had compassion enough to do any of these things for you. Rather, you were thrown out into the open field, for on the day you were born you were despised' (16:4, 5). Mixed parentage and foreign birth were followed by rough and crude dealings. The baby was neither cared for, washed, preserved against sickness, nor clothed. Thrown out and left to die, only by a miracle did she manage to survive. No one would find a child in this state particularly attractive, especially in the ancient world, where infant life was cheap. Israel heard God's reminder that there was nothing in her or in man to merit God's love. By ancestry and behaviour we have nothing about which to boast.

The grace of God in providence

At this crucial point, the Lord passed by and saw the infant, threatened by death and powerless to do anything, and grace said, 'Live!' (16:6.) Grace took this foundling and caused her to grow. She grew up and developed and became 'the most beautiful of jewels'. Everything was against survival, but the child not only survived, but grew to maturity and to beauty. I believe here we have a picture of the grace of God in providence that takes man in his sinfulness and keeps him alive to grow to maturity, despite the fact that in his spiritual need he is still 'naked and bare' before God (16:7). Every believer can remember times when life might well have ended, but we were spared to grow to maturity and

preserved until that time when the Lord came to meet
with us.

The grace of God in salvation

Years had passed and the rejected child had reached
marriageable age. Grace passed by again, not simply in
providence but now in the close relationship of love.
'When I looked at you and saw that you were old enough
for love, I spread the corner of my garment over you and
covered your nakedness' (16:8). The child, now grown, was
still naked; the Lord in his love not only made provision
to cover her nakedness, but in so doing expressed visibly
his offer of marriage. To spread clothing across a girl in
this way was equivalent to a solemn offer to marry her.
The Sovereign Lord took the sinful creature and entered
into this closest of all earthly relationships.

We have to notice that both in providence and in
salvation the initiative lay entirely with God himself. He
passed by, he saw, he spread his garment, he gave his
solemn oath and entered into a covenant. Grace did not
look for something attractive in the loved one, but was
prepared to look and choose and offer and give and to seal
it all with a solemn covenant. When we look at the cross
of our Lord Jesus Christ we see in him, not only provision
to cover the shame and nakedness of our sin, but also a
pledge to take us to be his own people in a relationship of
permanent love. Actions speak louder than words.

The immediate result was startling. The orphan girl
was first washed clean, then dressed in beautiful and
costly clothes. She was adorned with jewellery, with
bracelets and a necklace. Western cultures might not
appreciate the ring in the nose of 16:12, but some cultures
would see this as the crowning glory. But a crown was
given, too, together with tasteful earrings, silver, gold

and everything else needed to make her feel good and look beautiful. Her diet was immediately improved and she became very beautiful and rose to be a queen. We do not need to parallel every detail of this lovely picture, but the meaning is clear. The community of God's people, washed in the blood of Christ and made clean from her sin, is clothed in the robes of his righteousness, adorned with his beauty and sanctified by his Spirit until, exalted to his throne above, she reigns with him in glory. All of this is a result of the sovereign grace of God. He does the washing and the clothing, the beautifying and the crowning. We only contribute ourselves in our need and in response to his love.

As others watched the drama being performed before them, they began to take account of the fame of this new queen, 'because the splendour I had given you made your beauty perfect, declares the Sovereign Lord' (16:14). When the people of God is being what she was made to be, then those around sit up and take notice. At such times there is no need for the church to engage in gimmicks and entertainments to attract the people to her doors. Her own character is enough, with the glory of the Lord shining through. God sees to it that people are aware of what he has done. While the views of the world about the church are no infallible guide to her health, when she is right with God there is something irresistible about her, and when men ignore her as irrelevant we have a right to ask ourselves why.

The breach of promise

The Bible does not deal in fairy tales. And the end of this story of the cast-off who became a queen does not come at this happy-ever-after point. The story has only just begun. For the queen became familiar with her position and, little by little, and very subtly, her attention moved from her Lord to her looks. 'You trusted in your beauty,' says Ezekiel, 'and used your fame to become a prostitute. You lavished your favours on anyone who passed by and your beauty became his' (16:15). From centring her attention on her Lord, she began to look at herself and her possessions. Her self-confidence promoted pride and she began to think she was someone. The attention her attractions brought from others soon turned her head, and she wanted to be popular and accepted by them. So instead of giving thanks to her Master for his love and his gifts, she did the unthinkable and betrayed his love and loyalty by bestowing her favours on all and sundry. The Lord declares, 'Such things should not happen, nor should they ever occur' (16:16). He underlines the treachery by pointing out that the jewellery she turned into male idols was that which he had given her and it was made from 'my gold and silver'. The clothes draped round the idols and the provisions offered to them were all the gifts of God to his people. She used his own wedding dowry to finance her flirtations and adulteries. The crowning shame came with the offering of her infant children to inanimate blocks of wood and stone (16:20).

The history of Israel is replete with stories of her unfaithfulness to the Lord. Called to serve the Lord alone and to be his particular people, she was drawn time and time again by the desire to be like everyone else and to worship the gods of the surrounding areas, for fear that she might lose out. No one likes to be different. Yet the very word 'holy' derives its meaning from being set apart, and God called his people to be holy, to be different. Therefore the assimilation of Israel to the religion of her surroundings was not a minor aberration, but a terribly serious violation of her whole calling and relationship to the Lord. It was a fatal breach of promise in the love relationship.

The church of God has forgotten this lesson times without number throughout her history. She has forgotten that what attracts the world to her and to her message is not the measure in which she is the same as everyone else and offers to surrender her uniqueness and purity in exchange for popularity. Rather it is the unlike poles that attract, and the key to her drawing power is not her outward trappings and adornments and power, but her unique relationship to the living Lord of glory. Individual Christians forget this lesson, too. Subtly and gradually our affection turns inward from the Lord himself to the work he has done in us, and from trusting solely in his grace we begin to take confidence in the state of our sanctification. Then we move from difference to desire to be the same, and slowly sell out the love of the Lord for the love of the world.

How could Israel, how can we, sink so low? Her first mistake was one of forgetfulness. 'You did not remember the days of your youth, when you were naked and bare, kicking about in your blood' (16:22). When God's people forget their natural state, their original condition, dead in trespasses and sins, they begin to take the grace of God for granted. Short memories sire sins, and only a continual realization of what we owe to God can keep us from sinking back into complacency. Otherwise we devalue the cross and begin to wonder what all the fuss is about. Then we find ourselves at home in the world and adopt the values of the surrounding culture. We become so dulled in our sensitivities that we do not see how great a breach of promise this is, just as the faithless wife had become so used to all her possessions that she assumed they belonged to her by right and nature and not by gift and grace. A church or a people that has abandoned its allegiance to the Lord similarly assumes that its tawdry middle-class respectability is all there is to Christianity.

Alongside the forgetting went the losing of love and
devotion. The freshness and joy depart from a marriage
when a couple begin to take each other for granted. Love
and affection grow cold. Before long one of the partners
is looking outside for someone to bring the freshness in
again, and when they find that person they strike up a
new link with them. In so doing, they forget the natural
law of human relationships, which means the second
liaison will soon be taken for granted and the whole process will begin again. Israel fell into this trap with a
vengeance. Ezekiel spares no blushes in portraying her
cheap lust that offered itself without charge and was
even prepared to pay to hire a love. Every public square
featured its own brothel of spiritual adultery and the
head of every street proffered a lofty shrine to 'anyone
who passed by' (16:23–25). Even the surrounding
heathen nations were shocked by this crude display, but
Israel's appetite for adultery was insatiable and she
searched far and wide for new cults and new shrines to
include in her pantheon (16:26–29). 'Unlike a prostitute . . . you scorned payment . . . but you gave gifts
to all your lovers, bribing them to come to you from
everywhere for your illicit favours. So in your prosti-
tution you are the opposite of others; no one runs after
you for your favours. You are the very opposite, for you
give payment and none is given to you' (16:31–34).

This same process takes place every time the people
of God forget their position. The church that has lost
her first love for the Lord has little else to offer. From
being a throbbing centre of life she degenerates into
a club for the religious, those who lack the usual number
of red corpuscles to belong to ordinary human clubs
and find in the passivity of the church a support for their
weakness. In that condition the church becomes a pathetic
beggar, imploring others to like her and endorse her. She
goes around offering to sell any truth and give up any

standard, if only the world will love her. No one comes
after her, for she really has nothing to offer, so she
barters every position she should hold, and those with
whom she holds dialogue give nothing back in return.

The judgement of God

The punishment is made to fit the crime. Ezekiel portrays
the prostitute wife handed over to her many lovers, who
strip her bare, take her clothes and anything of value
and leave her with nothing (16:35–42). Far from showing mercy or delight in having her at their disposal, the
lovers she tried to attract despise her for her unfaithfulness. After they have taken everything of value they leave
her to rot. This indeed is the judgement of God on any
unfaithful church. Far from earning the respect of the
world, she is rapidly emptied of membership, spoiled of
her possessions and left to die out unmourned as a relic
of the ancient past. The salt that has lost its saltiness is
good for nothing but to be thrown out and trodden under
foot by men.

In 16:44–48, Ezekiel compares Judah with the already
destroyed kingdoms of Samaria and Sodom, both noted
for their evil ways. Judah looked down upon them as
corrupt, but Ezekiel shows that in fact she was worse
than they, sinning against a greater light and incurring
greater responsibility. The Lord Jesus himself heaped
greater woes still on Chorazin and Bethsaida because of
their even greater light. What must he think of us?
Interestingly too, the indictment of Sodom does not
focus on homosexuality, although elsewhere that is so,
but on complacency and indifference to social injustice
and the plight of the poor. 'Now this was the sin of your
sister Sodom: she and her daughters were arrogant, over-
fed and unconcerned; they did not help the poor and
needy' (16:49). Where do we find societies like that?

These passages underline again and again that the sin of deepest dye is not the crime of passion committed in the heat of the moment, but the fundamental breach of promise of a people who know they owe all to the grace of God and have tasted his love and have then thrown it all away as worthless. If decline in society begins with decline in religion, decline in religion reaches its bottom when the people of God sell his gifts to the lowest bidder and even try to give them away. A society that has a church like that is indeed in deep trouble. Judah had reached that stage and gone beyond it.

Hope still shines

But we have not yet reached the end of the story or the end of Ezekiel chapter 16. At this dark moment the Lord says, 'I will remember the covenant I made with you in the days of your youth, and I will establish an everlasting covenant with you . . . Then when I make atonement for you for all you have done, you will remember and be ashamed and never again open your mouth because of your humiliation, declares the Sovereign Lord' (16:60, 63). Grace cannot be quenched. Grace is sovereign, as sovereign as the Lord. All man's unfaithfulness will not finally be allowed to defeat the purposes of the living God. Grace will prevail in the end. Not that men will have no cause to be ashamed and to confess their unworthiness — rather the reverse, for they will be left with nothing to say. But we must not allow the bleak picture that stares at us from our Western societies today to make us so pessimistic that we feel all is lost. All is not lost, if we will acknowledge our sinfulness and if God in his grace will come and convict us of our sin.

As we reach the end of this section of the book, the picture is not pretty, but the diagnosis is honest. Decline in society begins with decline in religion. No matter how much people may protest that you can have morals without religion, that is not so, and if we persist in this error we shall have to see it written in the pages of history in letters of blood and misery. The problem is that we all soon become aware of decline in morals and increase in crime and all kinds of evil. We do not see so clearly when religion goes wrong. At first there is little effect in society; your spiritual capital remains and can be spent for the next fifty years. Who worries that the church buildings go empty and no one is listening to the preachers? They have had their day anyway. Only when the decline in religion spills over into other sectors of public life do we begin to see the fatal flaw magnified to a rift fault. That is what we will see in the next section.

9.
Comforted by Clichés

Somehow we all manage to go through life imagining that
'It will not happen to us.' Whether it is failing health,
a road accident, or final death, we have an inbuilt
mechanism that keeps us from applying to ourselves the
lesson of our own frailty. The leaders of Jerusalem were
just like that, indeed whole societies adopt the same stance.
They could not bring themselves to believe that their
precious society could possibly be threatened with
extinction or verging on catastrophe. Even the fact that
the cream of the population had disappeared into exile
a few years before failed to move the remnant that
remained. After all, they had been spared when the others
had been taken, so there just had to be something special
about them.

For Israel, the presence of the temple in Jerusalem stood
like a rock in the way of any suggestion that the city might
fall. God has given them that temple. The Holy of Holies
symbolized the very presence of God among them. How
could he possibly allow heathen hands to desecrate his
chosen place? So they lulled themselves to contented
apathetic sleep, convinced that God had favourites and
that they were the chief among them. In that context,
a disintegrating society comforted itself with clichés bearing
no resemblance to reality. Those clichés sound dis-
concertingly modern. In my early days as a curate in
London, I went hospital visiting each week, and by various
bedsides I used to meet the clichés of the day. 'It's all
right so long as you have got your health.' 'It will all work

out all right in the end.' Pious wishes or vain hopes with nothing to hang them on kept people from facing up to the stern realities of life.

'We have had crises before and we have muddled through. We will be able to do so again. Why make all the fuss?'
This was one of the common clichés of Ezekiel's day. People dismissed with scorn the merchant of doom and gloom. Yet he was speaking with justification. Arrogance blossomed in Israeli society. Violence had grown to alarming proportions, as 7:10, 11 indicate. Yet commercial activity went on as it had always done and will always do. The buyer went around rejoicing at his bargain and the seller at least pretended to mourn over his poor sale (7:11, 12). They saw no reason to shut down the market even for a day, simply because the political outlook was a bit gloomy. Yet the moral fibre had gone from their society, so that, despite the alarm that sounded, no one responded and the front lines were empty (7:14). When the crunch finally came, their hands went limp and their knees became weak as water. They expected it so little that they just could not cope.

As the enemy army fell upon the helpless crowd, the materialism that had so recently been the sole object of their attention suddenly emptied of value (7:19–22). People threw their precious silver into the mud of the streets, and the price of gold slumped to the level of the yellow dust it really was. Food became more valuable than a Swiss bank account, and jewellery only an object of plunder by the invading forces. Suddenly everyone wanted counsel. Frantically rushing around, they sought a vision from the prophet, teaching from the priest and counsel from the elders. But it was too late – the position was irreversible. When there was still time no one would listen. They had just expected that because they were the chosen people of God they could muddle through.

The most dangerous aspect of the whole picture is that
no one would take Ezekiel seriously. With the market
going full steam and the enemy a long way away, they
could see no earthly reason for concern. Heavenly reasons
did not interest them, so they ignored the warning clouds
and concentrated on making more money. Ezekiel buzzed
around like a nuisance of a fly in the summer time, something to be brushed away, a comma in the sentence of
commerce. How do you convince such a generation that
the living God cannot be ignored for ever, and that there
is a moral judgement to the universe? Any minister who
has tried to comfort the relatives of a dead person who
consistently left God out of his or her life knows how
hopeless that task is. Yet our Western societies as a whole
have turned their backs on any sense of answerability to
God, and when anyone tries to remind them about it,
the cliché comes back that muddling through has become
a workable principle of life that we do not intend to
change.

'It may happen to them but it will never happen to us'
This cliché with which I began this chapter is as old as the
hills! Chapter 11 shows that clearly. The Spirit lifted up
Ezekiel and took him from the refugee camp in Babylon
to the city of Jerusalem, where the leaders of Judah were
urging the population to believe in the future of their
city and country, and to invest in it. Despite the threatening political climate, they were firmly convinced that
nothing would happen to them. Their illustration sounds
foreign to our ears, as they talk about the city being a
cauldron and the leaders and people the meat. But the
meaning is clear. Despite the fire that licked around the
cauldron, the choice pieces of meat inside were protected
from being consumed by the solid iron of the pot.
Cauldrons were used for cooking the best meat, so they
obviously saw themselves as the choicest morsels in the

whole kitchen. That being so, it would soon be time to build houses, and investing in the local building society was one way to show confidence in the future of the country. Threats from outside or from the world scene could safely be ignored (11:2,3).

There seemed to be no limit to their self-confidence, for not only did they not see their own danger, but they also considered the exiles away in Babylon to be somewhat inferior creatures whom God was displeased with and had removed out of sight, leaving the land of hope and glory in the sole possession of his favourites. So the people of Jerusalem were saying about the exiled community, 'They are far away from the Lord; this land was given to us as our possession' (11:15). But in actual fact they had the whole thing the wrong way round. It was those in Jerusalem who were in imminent danger. The Lord's message thundered against the self-confident, declaring his intention to drive them out of their safe 'cooking pot', and expose them to the sword that they dreaded so much (11:7–12).

In the middle of this vision, just as Ezekiel was uttering the judgement, one of the key leaders in Jerusalem, Pelatiah son of Benaiah, dropped dead on the spot. A more dramatic underlining of Ezekiel's message can hardly be imagined. He himself was so shaken that he fell face down and cried out in a loud voice, 'Ah, Sovereign Lord! Will you completely destroy the remnant of Israel?' (11:13.) To the exiled community in Babylon, this dramatic event must have come with even greater force when it was later confirmed from Jerusalem that Pelatiah actually was dead. The Lord was not playing games.

This despised exilic community, far from being particularly rejected by the Lord, proved actually to be selected by him to escape the annihilation that Jerusalem was soon to experience. The Lord was 'a sanctuary for them in the countries where they have gone' (11:16). In

days to come, the Lord told them, 'I will gather you
from the nations and bring you back from the countries
where you have been scattered, and I will give you back
the land of Israel again.' These exiles would come back
purified from the syncretism of idolatry and after the
fire of suffering would possess a cleansed and uplifted
experience of God and a new obedience to his will
(11:18–21).

In our modern Western societies we have to be very
careful lest that self-confidence which is sure it can never
happen to us dominates our outlook, blinds our discernment and prevents our repentance. We are insulated by
our affluence from the fires of poverty, protected by our
armaments from outside dangers and separated by our
frontiers from some of the horrors of the modern world.
We can so easily look down on developing countries
struggling with the depths of poverty, wrestling with
the spectre of famine and disease and often writhing
under totalitarian regimes. We can see that they are in
trouble. We can look at Communist dictatorships and
pity those who dare not express their opinions, or even
know what is happening beyond their shores. We can
feel we are somehow the specially choice people of the
earth. After all, we enjoy democracy and affluence and
industrialization. We have a future in which to invest.
Surely the Almighty must be pleased with us.

In fact, the boot may well be on the other foot.
Spiritually, many countries outside the Western world
flourish in ways that highlight our poverty. In China,
Russia and Eastern Europe, the gospel spreads like wild-
fire despite every attempt to stop it. People in the depths
of suffering rise to heights of commitment and sacrifice
of which we know almost nothing. And in that climate
of hostility to faith, Christians experience such deep
fellowship that many would prefer to live under hostile
regimes than share our apathy. While in some of our

countries the church withers and dies, in theirs it grows and spreads. Does that not say something about the places where the grace of God is most at work? We may well be the people under judgement. We must not judge by outward appearances and present situations, for an atomic war could change all that in a few short hours. So we dare not use the cliché that it may happen to them, but it will never happen to us.

'Don't worry; it may never happen'

Here is another contemporary cliché shared by the man in the street in Jerusalem when Ezekiel was alive. Chapter 12 of his book shows that a proverb going around Jerusalem said, 'The days go by and every vision comes to nothing' (12:22). The prophets of doom and gloom have consistently been proved wrong, so why worry? Think of all those people who believed that the world was going to end on a certain day! Some of them sold their houses and followed some crank up to the top of a mountain, only to have to creep sheepishly home when the deadline passed uneventfully. Another popular proverb then was 'The vision he sees is for many years from now, and he prophesies about the distant future' (12:27). One day, of course, some fool will push the wrong button and the whole world will go up in smoke. If that never happens, eventually the earth will cool down so much that human life will become impossible. But, of course, neither of these things is likely to happen in our day, so why give it a second thought? People have always tried to scare us, and religious people have used the element of fear before to persuade people to follow them, but really there is no need to worry.

In that kind of situation, Ezekiel had to point out that there would come a time when something would really happen, and he was sure that that time was very near. ' "This is what the Sovereign Lord says: I am going to

put an end to this proverb, and they will no longer quote
it in Israel." Say to them, "The days are near when every
vision will be fulfilled"' (12:23,24). When God decides
to act, nothing can stop him.

Peter warned us that this particular cliché would be
popular at the end of human history. Scoffers would
come in the last days, 'scoffing and following their own
evil desires. They will say, "Where is this 'coming' he
promised? Ever since our fathers died, everything goes
on as it has since the beginning of creation"' (2 Peter
3:3,4). But Peter pointed out that people who talked
like that were ignoring the fact that the world has been
destroyed once already, by a flood. We might easily add
other illustrations. One of them would be Ezekiel's own
day, for not long after this prophecy Jerusalem was
destroyed and her people taken into exile. Again, Jesus
warned of the day when not one stone of the temple
would be left upon another, and in A.D. 70 that was
literally fulfilled. Of course, these were localized judgements, but they were just as much future events dismissed
beforehand as unlikely ever to happen.

Peter in his letter went on to point out that God's
time-scale is not ours, and one day with him can last a
thousand years or a thousand years be compressed into
twenty-four hours. Our knowledge of the vast time-scale
of the history of the earth should underline how differently God views time from the way we do. He also has
good reasons for delay. Peter brings these to our notice,
showing that, rather than being rooted in slackness or
hesitancy in executing judgement, they lie in his infinite
patience and grace, giving people every opportunity to
repent before the axe falls (2 Peter 3:9). Those who rely
on clichés like this one, that judgement will never happen
because it has not yet done so, are dicing with death and
throwing God's long-suffering goodness back in his face.
Delay was meant to produce repentance, not apathy.

Our generation is no different from the ones that went before. Many still have their heads in the sand, despite the ominous military and political rumblings. Like the residents of California, who happily live on the St Andreas fault despite the warnings of a big earthquake to come, we feel that if the earth is not actually falling apart at this moment it never will. We take refuge in the fact that war has not really touched Europe for nearly forty years, so we think our civilization is secure. Don't worry, it may never happen. As for the preachers who talk differently, they are a relic of a bygone age who have not caught up with the mood of the day. So people cosy themselves out of repentance and treat divine judgement as a joke, not a date on the calendar of history. Moving such people becomes almost impossible.

'Man is not morally responsible'

Another favourite cliché of Ezekiel's day combined complaint against God and excuse for man by declaiming responsibility. The proverb in this case was 'The fathers eat sour grapes, and the children's teeth are set on edge' (18:2). Children are not morally responsible. Why should they be blamed for the evil their father did? A child is the product of heredity. If his father was a criminal or unable to manage his own affairs, the child will grow up deprived. You cannot hold such a person responsible for growing up as he does, for to do so is to make him responsible for what his father was like, and that is manifestly unjust. So we excuse our failures as the result of our heredity. Maybe our parents were divorced, so how can we expect to make a success of our marriage? Maybe our father was an alcoholic, so it is not surprising if we have a problem with drink. In this way we take advantage of psychological theories to blame someone else for our own sins, and to excuse them as not really being sins at all, but congenital defects in our make-up.

If you add environment to heredity, you have a two-pronged excuse for anything wrong we may do and an alternative explanation to the sin of man for the state of our world. It is not that people are inherently sinful, but they have been brought up in a bad environment and inherited weakness from their families, so we must treat them not as morally responsible and accountable, but as the victims of their history and surroundings, and therefore to be pitied and treated as sick.

There is an element of truth in this, as in all clichés, otherwise they would not stand a chance of being believed. The problem arises when that truth is taken beyond proper limits and exaggerated into a theory that explains everything.

Ezekiel hammered home that, whatever our background, we are morally responsible beings and will be held accountable before God. 'The soul who sins is the one who will die' (18:4). When we look at others' sins we may legitimately see reasons why we should excuse them. When we look at ourselves we have to admit, 'I did it deliberately, freely and wrongfully. I am morally accountable.' Throughout chapter 18 Ezekiel examines all kinds of combinations of father and son, when the father is wicked and the son good, or the father good and the son wicked, and so on. The son of a wicked father is sometimes revolted by his father's behaviour and reacts against it by being totally different. Change is possible. The wicked man may repent of his sin and find forgiveness. The righteous man may stray from the right path. He is then morally responsible for doing so, and all his previous rightness does not in any way excuse him.

In other words, heredity (and to that we may add environment), are not the sole factors in determining the moral state of a person. Change is not impossible, and in fact does take place. Change can be for the better, as well as for the worse, and decisions taken can change the course of a life. Therefore to blame anyone else for the state of our own lives is to pluck an excuse out of the air that will not stand in the Day of Judgement. This particular cliché, that man is not morally responsible for his acts, is no more true than the rest of them.

We have already seen how the preachers of Ezekiel's day coddled the people in their sense of comfort and security, false though it was. Few things can destroy a people so easily as a sense of complacency, whether that be in matters of religion, politics, social welfare or economics. Material affluence coupled with and encouraging this comfortable way of life lulls men and women into the mistaken belief that what the world is today, it always will be. The frenetic rate of change with which we have to live does not seem able to blow away the fog. I live in Singapore, an island republic that has blossomed into affluence in little more than a decade. The speed of change in the last few years has exceeded the describable. Whole blocks of buildings disappear over-night, only to be replaced with bigger and better. But what worries the leaders of this modern miracle is the way it is possible for the next generation to take every-thing for granted. Young men going into the armed forces are now coming from much more sheltered backgrounds, and most young people have never known what it is to be in want or in danger. In such a climate clichés can prolifer-ate, and stimulating a population to awareness of threaten-ing dangers can be a hard task. In the West we have had this kind of problem for many years and it has multiplied. Societies comforted by clichés are in danger of disinte-grating, and while that subtle process may not be obvious at first, once begun it is very hard to reverse.

Ezekiel saw the process at work in Jerusalem, and by his day it had gone a long way. Yet still his people could not see it. So the Lord told him to sound the alarm as watch-man for his people, whether it was welcome or not.

10.
A portrait of decay

Jerusalem society was lulling itself to sleep with its
clichés – but what was really wrong with it? Were things
really so bad? If we take seriously the existence of the
God of history, we have to conclude that in fact they
were, for in a few short years Jerusalem was destroyed
and her people scattered in an act of divine judgement
which had been clearly announced beforehand. We
must then ask ourselves what were the roots and fruits
of the behaviour that made Judah's society so unacceptable. We find the answer in chapter 22 of Ezekiel. Here
we have a portrait of decay. The second verse designates
the basic roots from which Judah's decay sprung into
existence: violence and idolatry.

The Lord describes Jerusalem as 'the city of bloodshed', and 'the city that brings on herself doom by
shedding blood in her midst' (22:2,3). Violence had
become a way of life for many of her people. Quite
obviously we must not think of Jerusalem as one big
brawl, for there were victims of violence as well as those
who perpetrated it. Some no doubt longed nostalgically
for the time when it had been safe to walk the streets,
while others found themselves kicked around by the
powerful and the rich. Not everyone carried a knife, but
corporate restraints and public opinion were no longer
sufficient to prevent the violent and brutal from coming
out into the open. Time and again in history decaying
societies have been marked by the same fatal flaw.
A morally healthy society has sufficient inner strength

to restrain violence, but once that strength has been dissipated, might becomes right.

I need hardly describe the frightening increase in violent crime in many modern societies. Murder, rape and muggings keep people off the city streets at night and even sometimes in the day. Policemen patrol in pairs. Soccer hooligans rip through towns, breaking and bruising in senseless riot. Pickets and protests erupt into attacks, whether on authorities or bystanders. Old people tremble in their homes lest some gang of youngsters force their way in and bludgeon them to death for a few odd dollars or pounds. Our societies are made up of victims as well as offenders, too — that is not the point. The fact is that when these things reach a certain level, they are evidence of a sickness in society that we ignore at our peril. They indicate an advanced stage of decay.

The second root manifested in Judah's society was idolatry, for the Lord describes Judah as a city that 'defiles herself by making idols' (22:3). We have already seen evidence for this in other chapters. Judah had become just like any other people, adopting the gods of the locality lock, stock and barrel. Everyone around was worshipping at the latest shrine or on the nearest high ground, and not to join in was to be out of step, old-fashioned and rather to be pitied. Interestingly, the Lord describes Judah as 'guilty' over the violence and 'defiled' by the idolatry (22:4). Guilt called for retribution, but idolatry brought its own defilement, leaving the person and the society unclean. Nor were these two things unconnected. A society united in the worship of the one God has a common centre and common allegiance, but a society in which everyone does his own thing, which has no common centre beyond itself, but is dominated by a multiplicity of commitment to this, that and the other, is in danger of falling apart. Relapse into violence soon follows. Israel had lost her common allegiance to the

Lord, and her people were bowing the knee to every little local god who claimed power over the production of the crops in his own area. Their gods were too small to sustain the weight hung upon them. People become like the gods they worship, and when those gods are too small both their hopes and their society collapse. Idolatry raises petty objects to demand supreme allegiance and total commitment, when they are not worth such devotion. Sport and the stars of screen and scream could be reckoned as modern equivalents.

Ezekiel had to point out that the people of Judah were responsible for bringing upon themselves the situation they faced. They had brought doom upon themselves by shedding blood, and had defiled themselves with idols. So he told them, 'You have brought your days to a close, and the end of your years has come' (22:4). The responsibility was theirs. The Lord simply carried on what they had begun, and would make them 'an object of scorn to the nations and a laughing-stock to all the countries' (22:4). When we make fools of ourselves with idols, God makes fools of us to others. He does not have to do anything in particular to bring dishonour upon an idolatrous or violent society, for it carries within itself the seeds of its own destruction. God only has to leave us alone and we are well capable of destroying what previous generations have built. We then become an object of scorn and mockery to other nations. The West may be sought after for her scientific discoveries and technological experience, but she is not admired for her social decay. Her record in human rights may be better than socialist societies, but her freedom to sin speaks to them of disintegration. Developing countries may want her machinery but they would rather do without her morals. Other people can sometimes see that to which we are blind.

From the fact that Judah was marred at root by

violence and idolatry, we may learn that sin is not simply an individual matter. When prevalent in sufficient amount it invades the whole fabric of society. The body politic, like its human counterpart, has its own way of coping with the invasion of infection, but when it cannot produce sufficient antibodies to combat that intrusion, disease takes over and threatens the community's whole existence. Ezekiel spells out nine marks of the disease that had invaded Judah's life.

The first mark was *the wrongful use of power for selfish ends* (22:6). The princes of Israel were using power to shed blood. Instead of regarding it as a sacred trust to be exercised on behalf of those they governed, they saw it as a means to get what they wanted and to pursue their own ends. In recent years our world has not lacked such selfish leaders in some countries. The danger is always there, especially in societies where the breakdown of law and order could drive ordinary people to install in power a dictator who promises to remedy the chaos through strong-arm methods. Hitler came to power on just such a mood of total disillusionment.

The second mark was *the breakdown of parental authority*. 'In you,' he said, 'they have treated father and mother with contempt' (22:7). The breakdown of all forms of authority inevitably accompanies decline in belief in God. Unless authority is recognized as having been instituted by a higher power accepted by both parties, there is no logical basis for it. On the other hand, there is no restraint upon the person with sufficient power from assuming an unjustified authority. For example, the fact that I have brought children into the world and for some years I am stronger than they are does not provide any basis for my authority over them. But if God has given me that authority, then I have the right and responsibility to exercise it worthily and for the good of the child. In view of the decline in belief in God in many of our

societies today, it is not surprising that the breakdown of
parental authority is also rife. What is worse is that at
times even governments and leaders undermine the
authority of parents to an alarming degree. In England
a mother has been fighting for a long time against a
doctor's 'right' to issue contraceptives to her sixteen-
year-old daughter without informing the parents. The
courts have refused to uphold the parents' authority.
How strange that the same leaders who advocate such
practices also deplore the growth in juvenile crime
and hooliganism!

The third mark Ezekiel notes is that *'They have
oppressed the alien and ill-treated the fatherless and the
widow'* (22:7). Immigration poses problems for many
governments today in a world whose people wander more
and more frequently across the globe. Immigrants and
others seen as 'foreigners' become easy targets when a
community wants a violent outlet for its own frustrations.
Ezekiel was talking about minority communities and
defenceless people. The fatherless in Judah's society
had no one to stand up for them. The widows had no
union and often no income. The alien carried no political
clout; he could safely be left out in any consideration
of provision. Segments of society that are large or powerful enough to make their voices heard can usually compel
enough attention to ensure that they get some sort of a
fair deal. The real test of any society is not how it deals
with such pressure groups, but how it treats the people
with no voice and no power. The test also lies not in
what society does when minority or powerless communities start rioting and calling attention to their grievances,
but what it does for them when they are quiet.

The fourth mark of decay showed itself in *failure to
distinguish between the secular and the spiritual.* In fact
the spiritual side of life was thoroughly unpopular. 'You
have despised my holy things and desecrated my

Sabbaths,' complained the Lord (22:8). They had lost all reverence for anything connected with God and they treated one day in seven set aside for him as an unnecessary interruption in the life of business and pleasure. Unfortunately, certain 'with-it' priests only encouraged this trend. Verse 26 describes how these priests 'do violence to my law and profane my holy things; they do not distinguish between the holy and the common; they teach that there is no difference between the unclean and the clean; and they shut their eyes to the keeping of my Sabbaths, so that I am profaned among them'. For them the law of God could lightly be set aside as not being really relevant to the modern day. God had not meant what he said to be taken too literally and, in any case, he had said it in a different day and age, when people were not so enlightened. Distinction between the holy and the common was for them an unnecessary division of life, so rather than making everything holy, they recognized that the only thing to do was to make everything common. That would be more acceptable in a secular society. Wanting to impress their contemporaries with their understanding of their point of view, and wanting to attract more people to the temple worship when there were other more attractive shrines to attend, they lowered their standards so far that no one could see any difference any more. Every day was counted the same. Nothing could be labelled unclean and everything was permissible.

God clearly thought differently, and Ezekiel made it plain on whose side he stood. A society that has lost the ability to distinguish between clean and unclean is well on the way to failing to distinguish between right and wrong. Church leaders who fail to challenge this erosion of truth, but rather endorse every modern departure from it, incur the same wrath of God as Ezekiel pronounced on Judah.

The fifth mark is described in 22:9 as 'slanderous men bent on shedding blood'. *Character assassination was their trade and blood-shedding their badge.* Like the unscrupulous terror merchants of our day, for them the end justified the means. If the opposition could not be persuaded, then they had to be destroyed, either in their ability to hold their heads up in public through some vicious slander campaign, or through physical annihilation. Their ends formed the only criterion for life or death, libel or liquidation.

The sixth mark of decline is even more familiar to our generation. *All limits on sexual activity disappeared.* Promiscuity was actively encouraged and even given religious endorsement at the local shrines. All the lines once drawn were rubbed out and no new ones sketched in. Terrorists and slanderers joined their violent trade with their sexual adventures. Incest drew no condemnation; adultery and sex between close relatives knew no limits (22:10,11). Women were not safe. Nothing was banned. Sex is rather like loud music: the more you have, the more you want. Loud music is succeeded by louder music, until nothing louder is possible. So when sex is indulged it demands more and more unusual satisfaction, until nothing more can be found. At the same time, a train of misery begins that spreads from ruined individual lives through families that break up and on into a society that has forgotten what faithfulness means.

The seventh mark of decay showed itself in *criminal contracts to kill*. 'In you men accept bribes to shed blood' (22:12). When people get in the way of evil purposes, they become disposable. For the person who kills in a rush of anger, we can at least have some understanding as to why he might be pushed to the limit in this way. But the kind of murder in mind in this passage is cold-blooded and deliberate. The murderer sits and plans the whole thing, and carefully avoids any personal blame by employing someone else to do his dirty work. Society has now reached the stage where people not only plan murder like this, but those who want to can find someone willing to kill for cash.

The eighth mark comes in money dealings, with *ruthless exploitation* to make a quick profit. Excessive interest rates on loans and protection rackets against defenceless people provided an easy profit for those ready to use a little muscle. As 22:12 says, 'You take usury and excessive interest and make unjust gain from your neighbours by extortion.' I heard the following story recently about a business deal in Britain. A firm had made a contract with another business to carry out certain work. When the first firm's agent discussed the contract with the smaller man, he asked if he would be prepared to carry out other work which was not in the contract, and they would pay him for it. The second firm did the work, and then when it came to payment the first firm's agent refused to admit that he had asked for the extra work to be done and would not pay for it. On the way back to his office the agent boasted of the profit he had made for his firm by this deception. Maybe the smaller businessman should have been more careful, but quite clearly the agent had the swindle in mind in the first place. He had planned the profit on the way, but he had lost something more valuable – his own and his firm's integrity. This kind of thing abounds in a society marked by decay.

The final mark is not so much a mark in itself as another root cause of the whole process. *'You have forgotten me, declares the Sovereign Lord'* (12:12). A people aware of the unseen but living Lord, to whom they must individually and corporately render account, are restrained from using power selfishly, mistreating parents, violating holy things, practising terrorism and indulging in sexual licence. Criminal violence can only flourish where men have no sense of being answerable to a Power far higher than they are. When businessmen are aware of a Lord to whom they are responsible, integrity becomes more than a traditional conception. The society that bears the marks of social decay is also one that has lost all sense of the reality of God.

Perhaps this is the most alarming evidence of decay in Western countries. To talk of God has become an irrelevancy, an embarrassment. For most people it is taken for granted that such a Being, if he exists at all, only exists in the imagination of those who want to believe he is there; in any case he is harmless and certainly not concerned enough to get involved in what we are doing. Ezekiel wrestled with just such a situation. The very depth of his own experience of God, recorded in the first chapters of this book, made his contemporaries' carelessness all the more alarming. But in himself he was powerless to wake them from their dreams. He could only seek to bring them down to earth through his preaching and pray for God to convict them.

God's people must always be concerned about social decay. We dare not hide our heads in the sand or conceal ourselves in cosy communities, congratulating ourselves that we are not like other men, 'robbers, evildoers, adulterers — or even like this . . .' (Luke 18:11). We need to recognize the marks of decay and the extent to which they have already penetrated the body politic, and to be ready to take our stand on truth. There is no solution to such deterioration except in returning to awareness of God and being ready to repent and submit our lives to his scrutiny and our wills to his obedience. We need to sound the alarm even though we shall be caricatured as killjoys, wet blankets, doom and gloom merchants, and so on. We cannot produce an awareness of God by ourselves, but we can ask God in his grace to restore such an awareness to our people, and so begin to turn the tide of godlessness.

The size of Ezekiel's dilemma comes out in the closing verses of this chapter. Not only were there marks of decay within Jerusalem society, but they were manifested right through the social scale from the top downwards. Her leaders were no better than the ordinary people. The princes are called 'a conspiracy . . . like a roaring lion tearing its prey; they devour people, take treasures and precious things and make many widows' (22:25). We have already seen how her priests had lost any sense of distinction between the clean and the unclean, and simply endorsed the *status quo*. Her prophets were sellers of whitewash, ready to plaster their approval over any scheme the officials decided to implement. No wonder then that 'the people of the land practise extortion and commit robbery; they oppress the poor and needy and ill-treat the alien, denying them justice' (12:29). The pattern of behaviour came down from the leaders of society. Why should the leaders of society be allowed to grab all they can, and others be limited to keeping the rules? In this respect, many industrial societies have reaped what the early capitalists sowed. When the trade unions insist on grabbing all they can for their members, they are only following the bad example set for them. Why should they act responsibly if those who previously held the reins of power did not do so? So the vicious spiral sends society sliding down the scale.

As Ezekiel faced his own declining social structure in Jerusalem, he looked in vain for help. If only there had been someone ready to stand up and be counted! If only someone had been willing to say, 'The rot stops here'! But he looked in vain for such a person. The Lord put it this way: 'I looked for a man among them who would build up the wall and stand before me in the gap on behalf of the land so I would not have to destroy it, but I found none' (22:30). He reluctantly concluded that the only way forward was the way of judgement, 'so I will pour out my wrath on them and consume them with my fiery anger, bringing down on their own heads all they have done' (22:31). There was no delight in his voice — it was a knell of tragedy. Later on, the Lord Jesus Christ himself would look out on the same city and weep over it, with the cry on his lips: 'If only . . .' When he looks for people to stand in the breach in our society today, does he find anyone now ready to be counted, or is judgement the only way forward? We must not presume that we are the only people to whom these moral laws do not apply. Judgement could be nearer than we think.

11.
Caught in the storm

When the skies cloud over and the winds begin to blow, and the day we thought would be fine grows cold and threatening, we look for shelter, gather our clothes around us and hide from the elements, for we feel helpless to fight them. Those who live in regions where hurricanes or typhoons regularly threaten their existence know only too well the power of the storm. Ezekiel's Israel faced just such a storm, politically and socially. The feeling of helplessness must have been paralysing. How does the individual cope, when the mass of society around is bent on its own destruction?

We have seen the picture of the cloud, and that is underlined in Ezekiel by three other pictures which help us to face the dilemma of the individual. The first picture is seen in chapter 9, where the Lord calls for the guards of the city to come 'each with a weapon in his hand' (9:1). These guards are later sent through the city and told to kill 'without showing pity or compassion. Slaughter old men, young men and maidens, women and children . . .' (9:6), beginning with the elders of the people. Society had turned its back upon God and upon good, and the time of judgement had come.

The second picture covers chapters 9 to 11, and shows the glory of the Lord removing from the temple and gradually departing from the city completely. In 9:3 the glory moves to the threshold of the temple — a move seen again in 10:4,5 with an awe-inspiring description of the glory reminiscent of the vision of chapter 1. In

10:18,19 the glory of the Lord departs from the threshold of the temple and stops temporarily at the east gate of the Lord's house. At the entrance to this gate, twenty-five elders of Israel 'are plotting evil and giving wicked advice' (11:1,2). Ezekiel hears the Lord quoting against them their own parable of the cooking pot and showing them that, far from being safe like the meat in the cauldron, they will experience his judgement 'at the borders of Israel' (11:11). Finally, the cherubim spread their wings, with the glory of God above them, and move east of the city, evacuating it altogether (11:23). At that point the vision ceases and Ezekiel finds himself among the exiles again. Obviously the wickedness of the city and its leaders had reached the point of no return.

The third picture comes in chapter 15 and uses the familiar parable of the vine, a common picture of Israel. It is used in Psalm 80 to show God's grace to her and to plead for restoration of the vineyard, and in Isaiah 5 to show God's infinite care for the fruitfulness of the people and their utter ingratitude, in producing bloodshed instead of justice and cries of distress instead of righteousness. In Ezekiel 15 the vine has reached the stage of being good for nothing. The Lord comes to him and asks, 'How is the wood of a vine better than that of a branch on any of the trees in the forest? Is wood ever taken from it to make anything useful? Do they make pegs from it to hang things on?' (15:2,3.) The wood of the vine is good for nothing but burning. Unless a vine produces fruit it has no reason for existence, and the vine of Israel had ceased to produce anything like fruit towards God. The only course open to the Lord, therefore, was to commit her to be burnt in the fires of judgement.

For the individual caught in the storm, the future was bleak. What could one person do against such winds of change? Society had turned its back upon God, and the glory of the Lord was leaving the city. The vine had failed in its purpose, so what price the individual who really wanted to serve the Lord? Modern man knows this feeling of impotence, too, in the face of the ever-increasing threat of atomic war. What can one person do to avert catastrophe? And if society as a whole is determined to leave God out, what chance has the individual to stem the tide, or even make a difference? In the book called *Organisational Behaviour* by Fred Luthans[1], the author quotes a study by Melvin Seeman on 'The Meaning of Alienation'. He is referring not so much to the threat of destruction that hovers above us as to the impact of technology on our lives. He points out that the result on human psychology of the phenomenal increase of technology in recent years is a sense of powerlessness, meaninglessness, isolation and even self-estrangement. We have no resources with which to combat the inevitable tide of the times, and what is true of technology is also true of the arms race and of religious and social decline. Must we retreat into pessimism, or say with the world, 'Let us eat, drink and be merry, for tomorrow we die'?

Ezekiel and other Scriptures teach us that the Christian is neither without hope, nor without recourse to the Lord and his grace.

Christian concern is recorded and accepted

In chapter 9, before the guards of the city are sent out on their programme of destruction, a man clothed in linen, who has a writing kit at his side, is sent through Jerusalem to 'put a mark on the foreheads of those who grieve and lament over all the detestable things that are done in it'. Helpless they may be, but unnoticed they are not. In Revelation 7 we have a similar passage where the visitation of the angels in judgement is deferred until the servants of

God have been sealed on their foreheads (Revelation 7:3).
So, too, in Malachi 3:16,17, 'Those who feared the Lord
talked with each other, and the Lord listened and heard.
A scroll of remembrance was written in his presence
concerning those who feared the Lord and honoured his
name. "They will be mine," says the Lord Almighty,
"in the day when I make up my treasured possession."'
We cannot calculate the effect of individual concern in
a disintegrating environment. We do know that the Lord
takes notice of it, and that despite universal judgement
he makes a difference between the mass of people going
their own way and those who grieve over the situation.

Christian prayer and intercession are effective

We read little about Ezekiel's own prayer life or his feelings during his prophecies. Unlike Jeremiah, he does not
wear his heart on his sleeve and repeatedly express his
reactions. Chapter 9 is one of the few places where a cry
of concern is wrung from his heart. As he sees the guards
slaying the people of Jerusalem he falls down on his face
and cries out, 'Ah, Sovereign Lord! Are you going to
destroy the entire remnant of Israel in this outpouring of
your wrath on Jerusalem?' Again, in chapter 11, when
in his vision Pelatiah falls down dead before him, he cries
out with a loud voice, 'Ah, Sovereign Lord! Will you completely destroy the remnant of Israel?' (11:13.) Similarly,
in Revelation 8:3,4 the prayers of God's people are mixed
with incense and ascend to the throne of God, resulting
in God's activities upon earth. We do not know the effect
of the prayers of God's people. We do know that Ezekiel
and Revelation both teach very clearly that prayer does
have an effect, even upon a seemingly hopeless situation.
The day may be dark, but the Lord does hear.

Christian commitment is needed

Ezekiel points out in chapter 22 the tragedy of a society in which no one can be found to stand up and be counted. The Lord says, 'I looked for a man among them who would build up the wall and stand before me in the gap on behalf of the land so that I would not have to destroy it, but I found none' (22:30). We may feel that our witness is one against the crowd. What is the point of standing against an overwhelming tide? In the Lord's reckoning, the individual counts, even in a day when men discount him and his testimony. One person can make all the difference between life and death, disaster and deliverance. A day of deterioration is a day for boldness, not despair, a day for each one to take a deliberate stand for the Lord.

Christian response and welcome are honoured

Ezekiel himself does not mention this, but I feel that the situation facing the church in Laodicea is so closely parallel to Ezekiel's day and ours that it can be included here. There the individual is surrounded by lukewarm concern for the Lord and his work, and most people are wrapped in a mist of complacency that prevents their seeing their dire need. But the Lord himself comes to the individual, stands at the door and knocks, and invites all who will to admit him. To such he promises communion and fellowship and the right to sit with him on his throne (Revelation 3:19–21). When the crowd is lost in unbelief, the Lord still concerns himself in depth with those who are ready to respond.

As Christians in the modern world, we may often feel swamped by the circumstances that surround us and helpless to stem the tide. The visions of the first part of Ezekiel may make us feel even more helpless, but that should not be the case. It has often been said that one with God is a majority, and in a day when the individual is often helpless in the face of bureaucratic machines and proliferating arms races, we must remember that this is more than a cliché. God does take notice of each person.

12.
Turning-point — the blow falls

Mark the date on the calendar: today is the day. Ezekiel knew that morning that from now on everything would be different. The Lord told him to make this special note, to 'record this date, this very date, because the king of Babylon has laid siege to Jerusalem this very day' (24:2). We can all remember certain days that changed our world, if they did not change anyone else's. And some days hang in the memory like storm-clouds on a summer's day, quiet yet menacing; the very air stands still. I shall never forget the first sound of the air-raid warning when war was declared in 1939. The day was sunny and many friends had gone down to the beach. At 11 a.m. the fateful broadcast came through the old Echo valve radio in the sad and disappointed tones of a man whose political career had hinged on keeping the peace and who now knew it was all in vain. At ten years old I had no real idea what lay ahead in the next few years, but sufficient of the threat reached into my heart to strike terror there. Surely this was the end. The banshee wail of the siren only underlined the almost supernatural tension that surrounded us.

Ezekiel knew that for Jerusalem this was indeed the end, the end of threats and warnings and the coming of the judgement he had sought to avert. The talking had stopped and the action was about to begin. From this chapter we understand that the Lord gave Ezekiel special advance warning of what was happening hundreds of miles away. There was no phone or telex to communicate the disaster, but Ezekiel knew the very day it began. He was then given a message to convey to the exiles in Babylon, those who were holding on to the vain hope that Jerusalem would never fall and that they would be back home in a few months or years at the most. In chapter 11:3 the leaders of Jerusalem had used the picture of the cooking pot to express their own self-confidence. They themselves were inside the pot, the choice pieces of meat, protected from the fire outside by the solid metal of the cauldron. Now Ezekiel used the same symbol, explaining that they were indeed the meat inside the cooking pot, but the pot was going to be brought to the boil and even the bones would be cooked (24:3,4). The pot was encrusted and the pieces of meat would be taken out one by one to be exposed to the judgement of God on their violence (24:6–8). The heat would be on and the bones would be charred, the cauldron itself glowing with the heat, but even so the impurities in the metal would frustrate every effort to bring purification. Violence and impurity had so impregnated the social life of Jerusalem that the Lord had to say, 'The time has come for me to act. I will not hold back; I will not have pity, nor will I relent. You will be judged according to your conduct and your actions' (24:14). This time there was no going back.

Are we in any better position? Christians do sometimes take an unnecessarily gloomy picture of society around them, forgetting to see that which is good and positive. Our belief in the second coming of the Lord Jesus Christ and the reality of God's final judgement can make us interpret the signs we are given to mean this judgement is imminent. But many generations have done so, and the end has not yet come. So we have to be careful. Yet at the same time we must not pass over those signs, or pretend that because judgement is postponed it will never arrive.

As I look at Britain today my heart has to tremble for her. The parallels with Ezekiel's Jerusalem are too strong

for me to be able to dismiss them with a wave of the hand.
By and large as a nation we live as though God had no
more real existence than Father Christmas. Indeed, the
forces of unbelieving humanism and active Satanism are
not only present, but militantly active to destroy what
remains of Christendom. Large sections of the church
have no voice to raise against these attacks. The twin
symptoms of violence and sexual licence have invaded
society to the point where a turn of the tide appears
almost impossible. If Jerusalem merited judgement, I have
to ask myself why we should be spared.

The message of judgement is today the lost chord in the
church's music. We have left the trumpet and the other
brass out of the score, the tympanist has taken a break
and we are playing the light sound of the strings until
people are tired of it.

How did Ezekiel feel on that day? He would have
been entitled to turn round on the false prophets and say,
'I told you so.' But to be right about judgement brings
no delight to the true servant of God, for we still belong
to our people. The pathos deepens when we realize what
the fall of Jerusalem meant for Ezekiel's own family
circle. The man who spoke as the voice of God was about
to experience in his own heart the grief not only of his
people, but of the God of judgement himself. Ezekiel's
wife was going to die. 'Son of man, with one blow I am
about to take away from you the delight of your eyes'
(24:15).

Quite obviously, Ezekiel loved his wife. She was the
delight of his eyes. Yet, just as Jerusalem was about to
die, so was she. He spoke to the people in the morning
and discharged his responsibilities through the rest of
the day 'and in the evening my wife died' (24:18). We
can imagine how he felt during that day. We can feel
his apprehension, sense his pain and understand his long-
ing to be able to avert the blow. We may ask ourselves

why God should allow such a terrible thing if indeed he
is a God of love, but when we do so we betray our own
lack of understanding of his heart. We are failing to see
that he does not delight in judgement, that he feels the pain
of such blows and that he wants his servants to identify
both with his pain and that of the people to whom we
minister. We are not to be unfeeling preachers of God's
words and judgements, but to share the depths of the
sufferings of our world and our people, and to know the
depths of the sufferings that our God also feels. George
Whitefield is quoted as saying that if a minister can speak
of hell without tears in his eyes, he should not speak of
it. Ezekiel knew what this meant; he felt that pain of the
loss of his wife. And God felt the pain of his own Son's
suffering and death as on the cross he bore the sins of the
whole world that we might be spared the final judgement
of God. We cannot expect to be exempt. The gospel is
not a soothing ointment to magic away our sorrows, but
strong medicine to deal with very deep problems. And at
the centre stands a cross.

Ezekiel's suffering deepened when the Lord spoke to
him again, telling him, 'Do not lament or weep or shed
any tears. Groan quietly; do not mourn for the dead. Keep
your turban fastened and your sandals on your feet; do
not cover the lower part of your face or eat the customary
food of mourners' (24:17). Many of the customs of
Ezekiel's day sound strange to us, but obviously God was
telling him to behave as though nothing had happened.
That really does sound cruel. Yet when we understand
the position of the exiles in Babylon we can see what
God was doing. The loss of Jerusalem would be as big a
blow to the exiles as the death of his wife was to
Ezekiel. Yet they dared not mourn for the fall of Jerusalem
in the capital of the very country that was celebrating it
as a major victory! To be seen mourning would be to
invite reprisals from the people and government of Babylon

(see 24:19—24). Ezekiel was called to act out their circumstances in his own family life, so he, too, must not mourn
the loss of his wife. God's servants are not only called to
warn of judgement to come and to plead with people to
repent before it is too late; they are also called to identify
with those same people in the hour of their judgement.
He who would be of any real use in this world must identify with God in his holiness and also with people in their
sinfulness, at the same time keeping himself free of the
sin that clogs their lives. Only Jesus filled this role
perfectly, but we are called to walk in his steps.

It is important to remember that all this happened to
Ezekiel before the news filtered through from Jerusalem
that the city had actually fallen. The final proof that he
had been sent by God would arrive in the form of a
messenger bringing the fatal news. Then he would be a
sign to his people 'and they will know that I am the Lord'
(24:25—27).

Throughout chapters 25—32 the world seems to hold
its breath, while Ezekiel gives his attention to the sins and
problems of surrounding countries like Ammon, Moab,
Edom, Philistia, Tyre, Sidon, Egypt and even Babylon
itself. In these chapters the Lord is shown to be Lord of
all nations and no respecter of persons, of military might
or economic strength. We do not have the space to deal
with these oracles, for our mind is on Jerusalem. Chapter
33 takes up her story once again.

'A man who had escaped from Jerusalem came to me
and said, "The city has fallen!"' (33:21.) He did not
need to say any more: some news needs conveying in a
minimum of words. Ezekiel already knew what was coming,
for the evening before 'the hand of the Lord was upon
me, and he opened my mouth before the man came to me
in the morning' (33:22). The message he now had to
convey was a warning against facile hopes and superficial
answers, even if they were seemingly backed by Scripture.

The people were already saying, 'Abraham was only one man, yet he possessed the land. But we are many; surely the land has been given to us as our possession' (33:24). There were people back in Israel and among the exiles, picking themselves up out of the ruins and still clinging to vain hopes. God's answer silenced their expectation with a reminder of the twin causes of their downfall in violence and promiscuity, linked with idolatry. 'Should you then possess the land?' Their reliance on Abraham and his example had no basis in reality. True, Abraham had been only one man, but he had been a faithful and obedient one. They were neither. True, Abraham had possessed the land, or rather his descendants had four hundred years later. But God had promised to give the land to him, whereas God had told this people that he was taking it away from them.

Sometimes evangelical teachers and leaders are guilty of the same kind of blind optimism that bears no relation to reality. I remember hearing one prominent Christian leader publicly and confidently prophesying that during that summer, through his organization and the activity of short-term workers and national Christians, one million people would believe in Jesus Christ in Thailand. This was in spite of the fact that, after 150 years of the ministry of faithful servants of God, Christians in Thailand still number only just over fifty thousand in a country of forty-nine million. Blind optimism is not faith. Faith responds to the substance of God's promises and Word, not to the confidence of our predictions. The people of Ezekiel's day were in danger of trusting figments of their imagination, and Ezekiel had to disillusion them. We do not commend the gospel by pretending that what we would like to be will be. The gospel is more than the power of positive thinking.

One effect of the fall of Jerusalem may have come to Ezekiel as a pleasant surprise, although it did not last long. He suddenly found himself popular. From being the black sheep of the ministry he was suddenly shown to be the only one in step, the only one to get things right. Everyone else had said Jerusalem would not fall, but he had stuck to his viewpoint and said that it would. Now it was the other side's turn to have red faces, and everyone was talking about Ezekiel and what a wonderful preacher he was. 'Your countrymen are talking together about you by the walls and at the doors of the houses, saying to each other, "Come and hear the message that has come from the Lord"' (33:30). They admired his oratory. Indeed, his preaching must have been something special, for they likened it to 'one who sings love songs with a beautiful voice and plays an instrument well'. But even in this there was a jarring note. The people admired his delivery, and the accuracy of his prediction was temporarily popular. But that was as far as their response went. They had no intention of changing their ways or allowing the Word of God to make any impact on their life-style or culture. 'My people come to you, as they usually do, and sit before you to listen to your words, *but they do not put them into practice.* With their mouths they express devotion, but their hearts are greedy for unjust gain . . . they hear your words but do not put them into practice' (33:31,32).

Nothing grieves the heart of the true man of God more than to have people congratulating him on his sermon and saying how much they enjoyed it or received blessing from it — only to find that the effect of the Word of God on their lives is precisely nothing. What is the use of good preaching if it does not change lives? The saddest part of the revival of born-again evangelical religion across the world today is its lack of impact upon the way Christians live.

In Ezekiel's day the people really worshipped materialism. Their hearts were on their gain, and they were not fussy how they made it. Our real religion manifests itself not on Sunday in church, but on Monday to Friday in the market-place or the home. What we do in church may be limited to mouthing the right things and hearing what someone has to say, but what we do through the week expresses what we really believe. Hearing God's Word without allowing it to affect our lives is worse than honestly saying we do not believe any more. Church growth without changed behaviour is a recipe for disaster.

And so Jerusalem fell and the hopes of the refugees collapsed. But was Israel finally finished? This chapter not only marks the end of an era, but also the beginning of a new one. So far we have been majoring on the problems, sins, failings and disasters of God's people. We have to do that, for we must not pretend all is well when it is not. But although Ezekiel's opening vision began with a threatening cloud looming over his people, we must not forget that the cloud also had a silver lining. His book is not all doom and gloom. This chapter presents a kind of fulcrum on which the forces of God turn. From now on we may begin to look at the brightness of God's answers to the depths of man's failures. The day is beginning to dawn.

The silver lining

13.
A new ruler

The cloud in the sky had dominated Ezekiel's first thoughts as he wandered outside the refugee camp, and the cloud of threatened judgement darkens the first part of his book. Chapter 34, however, marks the beginning of change. The silver lining of God's purposes starts to shine through the gloom, until the brightness of his future plans bursts through and the promises of grace once more lighten the scene.

The dawn of a new day begins with the picture of a new kind of rule for the peoples of the earth. Responsibility for the deterioration of society has to be laid at the door of accountable leaders, and in Judah and Israel these rulers had failed. In depicting a new kind of society to come, therefore, the Lord begins with a new kind of ruler.

Chapter 34 of Ezekiel brings a prophecy against the shepherds of Israel, and we need to realize that the picture of the shepherd in the Bible is not simply a pastoral one, but also depicts those who rule. God's ideal for his people was for rulers concerned for the welfare of the people whom they governed, and therefore the pastoral side of the picture is relevant to the subject of government. In any case, in a theocracy, the rulers were in fact the pastors of society. How did they fail?

They cared for themselves

The primary responsibility of the shepherd was to care for

the flock. The main aim of Judah's leaders was to keep
themselves in office and to further their own ends (34:2).
The danger any politician faces is that he can be removed
from office, so he is tempted to give attention to schemes
that attract support rather than to projects that further
the welfare of the people. The two kinds of programme
may well conflict. The very possession of power is a
temptation to use it to attain selfish ends, and they are
strong people indeed who resist such temptation. The
leaders of Judah made sure that they received all the
benefits of being in office. They had the best food and
wore the best clothes. They were familiar with expense
accounts and vehicles that went with the job, but when
it came to caring for the people they lost interest (34:2).

They used power to keep the people in their place

Weak members of society received scant attention. The
sick had to provide for themselves. The drop-outs and
those who could not cope were left to wander their way
through life. The important thing from their point of
view was to teach the people who was in charge and to
put down any opposition. The inevitable result of this
kind of approach to government was harshness and
brutality (34:4). We see the same syndrome in modern
societies. The less concerned a regime is for the real needs
of its people, the more it has to be shored up by secret
police and strong-arm methods. Throughout history auto-
cratic monarchies, left and right wing dictatorships and
tyrannical regimes all tell the same story.

The people had no sense of purpose

Indeed the people lay at the mercy of any and every

exploiter. With no one to stand up for them, the ordinary people had no recourse when pushed around by the strong or the powerful. They could only move somewhere else and suffer at the hands of someone else. The result was a loss of cohesion in society, a dissolving of those ties of kindred and locality that bind a community together. No one bothered when someone disappeared from view. No one sought out those who had lost their way or their security. Bad government leads to an aimless people who have lost interest in life. No one feels that they are going anywhere (34:5,6). Such government, the Lord informed Ezekiel, was only fit to be replaced. The Lord was against these ineffective shepherds. He would hold them account-able and remove them from their positions (34:10).

This century has seen government after government of self-centred rulers deposed and replaced, only to be followed by something little better or much worse. New forces have taken over in country after country, making bright promises about the elimination of corruption and the dawn of a new day for the poor and needy, only to become just like the old forces they replaced. We can easily become cynical about politics.

Yet the Christian believer must never become a cynic. God is not, and he constantly holds out the promise of better things to come. Yet God is also a realist, for he knows the human heart and the sin that corrupts not only human lives but human structures. So the promise of Ezekiel 34 is that one day the Lord himself will take over the reins of government and the world will see how leadership was meant to be exercised. He sets out his pattern for ideal government in 34:11–31.

Good government cares for the people and draws them together

The Lord says that he will 'search for my sheep and look

after them'. He will reverse the trend that sends people
wandering, gathering them together and uniting them
in a healthy community in their own land and seeing that
they are provided for (34:11–14). His concern is not
for himself, but for his people. As the Good Shepherd
himself said upon earth, 'The good shepherd lays down
his life for the sheep.' He is not concerned with his own
power and position but with his people's welfare.

Good government cares for the lost, the weak and the sick

Chapter 34:16 portrays the shepherd going out to look for
the lost. In any society there will always be those who
lose their way in life. They are the misfits, the awkward
ones, the rejects, who are so difficult to rehabilitate. They
consume time and resources and contribute little, but in
God's eyes they are to be a prime concern of those in
authority. They certainly provide little political capital
and therefore are usually neglected until their life-style
forces attention and often invites reprisals. Similarly,
the injured and the weak take time and attention and
may never give very much in return, but to the Lord
they are key members of society calling for care.

Good government restrains the strong and rules with social justice

'The sleek and the strong I will destroy,' says the Lord.
'I will shepherd the flock with justice.' The sleek and
the strong in this case appear to be those who have taken
advantage of their position of power to oppress the people
and claim an unfair portion of resources for themselves.
God does not approve of that kind of selfish activity and

is concerned to shepherd the flock with justice. Care for
the casualties of society and correction of abuses of power
are therefore high on his list of priorities. The strong are
well able to look after themselves, and government should
therefore be concerned with assisting the weak and curbing
the excesses of the strong.

Good government limits the exploitation of resources

The Lord says that he will judge between one sheep and
another and between various kinds of sheep and goats.
He is distressed by those who not only eat the best themselves, but 'also trample the rest of your pasture with your
feet'. Their selfish exploitation did not limit itself to
securing the purest water for themselves but involved
muddying the rest with their feet (34:18,19). We are very
familiar in our day with the problems of pollution and the
ruthless exploitation of resources that not only gives some
sections of the world and of particular societies an unfair
share of resources, but also poisons the ecological system
for everybody. The kind of government the Lord brings
with him puts an end to such exploitation.

Good government is concerned for the needs of the poor

The Lord in his manifesto declares that he will judge
between the fat sheep and the lean ones. He will put an
end to 'shoving' and 'butting' that leads to the poorer
people being driven away and plundered. His one shepherd,
'my servant David', will tend them and be their shepherd
(34:20–23). He certainly does not seem to approve a
completely *laissez-faire* economic system, but sees the

responsibility of the ruler to act as judge between different sections of society, restraining the use of power and force in the interests of the underprivileged.

The effect of such a good government leads in the closing verses of the chapter to the picture of an ideal society, where not only have the social problems been dealt with, but an ecological balance has been restored, affecting the climatic conditions as well as the political ones. Under the direction of the Creator, not only does human life become peaceful, but the whole of the creation works as it was intended to do (34:25–31).

The world longs for this kind of government and society, where justice reigns and peace prevails. Neither the capitalism of the West, nor the Communism of the East can be said to have come anywhere near the ideal. Communism raised great hopes in the minds and hearts of many, for it seemed that here at last was an alternative based on social justice and the limitation of the powers of the strong. Some Western theologians even argued for some years that in China the kingdom of God had at last arrived and that God was clearly at work, not so much in the church as in the Communist experiment. Recent events have dissolved such hopes into disillusionment. The appalling excesses of the cultural revolution and the distressing effects of this on Chinese society and economic progress are too well known to leave any illusions that Communism has the answer for them. The revelations that have come out of Russia through people like Solzhenitsyn have likewise opened the eyes of all but the most deliberately blind to the failure of atheistic Communism there. And as if that were not enough, the genocide in Cambodia and the boat people fleeing from Vietnam have carried their own message that Communism simply exchanges one form of oppression for another. Nor can capitalism pretend to have solved the problems of the underprivileged and the weaker segments of society.

Indeed the whole economic scene is dominated by the awful spectre of the world's poor people getting poorer and poorer, while the rich get richer and richer.

This chapter in Ezekiel carries an important message for Christian believers as they look out on a world like ours, facing increasing despair and worsening problems.

1. Human systems of government will never succeed in establishing an ideal world of social justice and true peace

That may seem to be a cynical conclusion, but it is not that — only a realistic one. The sooner that we acknowledge that our problems are beyond our own capacity to solve, the sooner we will be prepared to submit to the Lord's own rule. Our determination to solve our own problems in the political and social realm is only our determination to run our own lives in independence of God, writ large. Sin entered the Garden of Eden when Adam decided that by taking the forbidden fruit he would be able to run his own life in total independence of God. Only when he reaches the point of despair in being able to do that does man begin to turn to God himself for his salvation and deliverance.

The history of man is long enough to show that successive utopian schemes have all foundered on man's own selfishness. Communism is only the last in the long list. Any plan built on an idealistic view of the goodness of man is bound to collapse in the end, for it is based on a lie. The human heart is very proud and refuses to admit its need, but Christian believers know that man's bent is self-centred and until human sin is eradicated there cannot be an ideal society. God has said so. History teaches us so. Therefore the Christian will view all man-made schemes for Utopia with a healthy scepticism and will not identify completely with any such scheme. They are all bound to fail.

2. Only the return of Jesus Christ as Lord will bring in the ideal society

We see the pattern of ideal government foreshadowed for us in the life of Jesus Christ upon earth. He was the Good Shepherd who laid down his life for the sheep. He was the Lord and Master who took a towel and washed his disciples' feet. He was the ruler who was also a servant. He spent his time, not in the corridors of power, but in the homes of the humble and in the fields of the peasants. He challenged the vested interests and healed the sick, sought the wandering and restored the fallen. The King of Israel inaugurated a new style of rule, symbolized for them and for us in his riding into Jerusalem, not in a Cadillac or chariot, not in a Daimler, but on a donkey.

Therefore only when this Son of David comes back to reign in accordance with Ezekiel 34:23,24 will we see a perfect system of government. Then he will rule with a rod of iron and all men will submit to his discipline. Power will not corrupt him, because as the sinless Son of God he cannot be corrupted. He is therefore the only one who can be trusted with absolute power. He is not interested in his own power structure — he does not have to be, for it is totally secured by the Lord himself. He is not interested in pleasing himself. He gave his life for the sins of the world. He is not going to change when he rules the world.

Christians are realists. They are not looking for a pie in the sky when they die, but accept our world as it actually is constituted. The world was made by God, therefore God must be acknowledged. Man fell from innocence into sin, therefore all human institutions hold within themselves the same fatal flaw. Jesus Christ came to this earth, lived and died and rose again to deal with human sin and to claim the throne of the universe. Therefore it stands to reason that only a system of government of which he is the Head can possibly succeed in ruling this world properly. While therefore the world may think us mad, the newspaper headlines prove us right in the negative sense of revealing the bankruptcy of every other alternative; we are prepared to wait for the end of history to demonstrate the positive side of God's answer.

3. *As responsible human beings we will attempt to produce the best kind of society of which human nature is capable*

Sometimes Christians behave irresponsibly. We congratulate ourselves on the rightness of our diagnosis and use it as an excuse to contract out of the world around us. But that is to deny our part in the human race. Ezekiel's conviction that the rule of God must come if society was to be governed properly did not keep him from calling attention to the wrongs of his own community and endeavouring to put them right. We may be convinced that no special programme of reform will usher in the ideal society, but we should have convictions about where our own society should be going.

That does not mean we should have a Christian political party. That is a dangerous thing. The programme of such a party inevitably becomes identified with the Christian viewpoint, but no one party viewpoint has all the answers. Furthermore, every political party is subject to the failings of human nature and will manifest them in its own programmes and in its personal relationships within the party. To attach the name of Christ to such programmes results in the name of Christ being dragged unnecessarily into the dust of political infighting. We need Christian politicians, but we need them in many groups, acting as salt and light in the context of their own parties. Then the whole of society may know the restraining and challenging hand of the Spirit of God in his people.

In this matter Christians face the same tension that confronts them at every turn. They are members of earthly

kingdoms and societies, but they are also children of the
kingdom of God. They live on this earth, but they look
for the world to come. They realize the failings of this
world and the sinfulness of human nature, but they look
with hope to a new world in which righteousness can
make her home. Ezekiel encourages us in this chapter
to lift up our heads in anticipation. The coming of the
King and the kingdom of true social justice cannot be
long delayed. We need not be ashamed of our 'other-
worldly' expectations. They are the only ones with any
hope of fulfilment. In the meantime, we will give ourselves to introducing the standards of that kingdom into
the kingdoms of this world. Our future hope is the motive
that drives us to involvement.

14.
A new heart

Sin wrecks every human attempt to create the ideal society. So long as human beings are incurably self-centred, they will not co-operate with each other beyond certain limits. So long as there is no supreme authority recognized as above the human race, people will not submit to each other unless they see personal advantage in doing so. Working together calls for limitations on our desires, restrictions on our freedoms and readiness to yield ground to each other. Since the Fall in the garden of Eden we have all wanted to make our own decisions, govern our own lives and live according to our own impulses. Not only so, but as Christians we recognize the reality of the supernatural world and of malignant forces working to subvert God's plan. Our contemporaries may dismiss them as relics of a superstitious age, but we cannot explain many happenings in our world realistically in any other way. Why, for instance, do efforts by seemingly sincere leaders to achieve peace in places like Lebanon never come to anything?

Evolutionary theory, applied to every discipline under the sun, persuades sociologists that man is getting better and better. The facts speak differently. We know much more than our fathers, we can go much further than they did, but we behave no better. They used bows and arrows to shoot each other out of the way; we build tanks and guns, missiles and chemical weapons. In any other area of study the scientific method would compel men to admit the truth, but when the subject of study is man, we lose our objectivity and escape into fantasy. We believe what we want to believe.

Ezekiel was a realist because he was in touch with God. We are not surprised to find, therefore, that in chapter 36 of his book Ezekiel moves from the need of a new ruler to the need for new people. For centuries Israel had filled the role of God's chosen people, his pilot project of a community under his direction, kept by his promises, guarded by his power and intended to live according to his will. The law provided a basis for living far in advance of the surrounding communities. But sinful human nature managed to wreck the project and throw God's grace back in his face. Therefore simply to provide Israel with a new divine ruler would not solve her problems. Nor would it solve ours.

If Jesus Christ came back to rule this world tomorrow, the only way in which he could persuade humanity to accept his standards and his kingdom would be to run a kind of police state. Most, if not all, vested interests would object to his interfering in their monopolies or power structures. Promiscuous people would complain of limitations on their freedom to fornicate or commit adultery. The Gay movement would protest in the streets. The speculators would prophesy the ruin of the economy. Every sinful human being would find his liberty infringed. The only way to run such a kingdom would be by force. The devil offered that kind of solution to Jesus long ago in the wilderness, and Jesus turned him down flat. The only real way to promote a new rule of righteousness is to produce new people who welcome it.

From the human point of view, the Lord's pilot project with Israel failed to produce the kind of community required. From the divine point of view this was no surprise, but part of God's purposes in educating the human race in his supreme plan. Man's failures never frustrate the purposes of God in the end. However, the

Lord fully understood that from the viewpoint of the nations surrounding Israel, his judgements upon Israel were their opportunity for plunder. They were not slow to take advantage of it. So Edom 'with glee and with malice in their hearts . . . made my land their own possession so that they might plunder its pastureland' (36:5). The world laughs in scorn when the people of God go down.

Yet God has not changed his mind about producing a people for himself. The destruction of Jerusalem was a comma in his story. In 36:8—12 he clarifies his purpose to produce a fruitful land and a fruitful people, settled and prosperous and more numerous than before. The world around described the promised land as one that devoured its people and robbed them of their children, but the Sovereign Lord was going to change all that (36:14,15). Yet he also faced a dilemma. The conduct of Judah required God's judgement if the moral basis of the universe was to have any meaning. But this judgement opened the way for others to say that the Lord was incapable of defending his people, and had in fact let them down. Either way, therefore, the glory of God and the purity of his name could be dragged in the dust. The people themselves had profaned his name by their behaviour, and now others were saying, 'These are the Lord's people, and yet they had to leave his land' (36:20).

God's answer vindicated the holiness of his name but restored his people to their position through a combination of judgement and grace. On the one hand, the judgement of God had fallen upon Jerusalem for her sins. On the other hand, out of the ruins the Lord would raise up a new people, cleansed from their sins and given a new nature through the implantation of the Spirit within their hearts. Judgement had come; grace was yet to come. The new day would be matched by a new people, a new creation.

So in 36:24–32 God's purposes are unfolded. The people would be gathered out of the nations, brought into their own land and made clean from past sins and impurities. To eliminate the basic flaw in sinful human nature, the unyielding and unresponsive heart of stone would be replaced by a new heart and a new spirit that senses and feels and responds. God's own Spirit would come to dwell in men and women and he would move them from within to respond to his will for their lives. As a result the land would become fruitful and judgements would be withdrawn. The people themselves would also recognize their former sinfulness and acknowledge that God's dealings flow from free, unmerited, purposeful love.

To whom do these verses apply? Some will tell us that they apply to a restored Israel, back in Palestine and returning back to God. That may be a part of the truth, but I cannot believe God only had that in mind when he caused this passage to be written. I do not think that the God of the Bible satisfies man's insatiable curiosity about the future in the way science fiction does. His word to man is profitable for teaching, rebuking, correcting and training in righteousness now (2 Timothy 3:16). His aim is to equip the man of God for every good work, not simply to give him an insight into coming events. So this is one of those many passages of Scripture which apply to more than one set of circumstances and may have more than one fulfilment. They may well apply to the people of Israel, but they describe the impact of the gospel so accurately that we have to apply them to God's action in creating a new people by his grace.

In dealing with the whole human race, God faced the same dilemma that he did with Israel. Man in rebellion deserved nothing but judgement; God in love wanted to restore man to his former position. To withhold the judgement for no reason would be to overthrow the moral basis of the universe; to execute the judgement would eliminate the object of the divine love. In the cross of Jesus Christ God himself provided the answer, as through his death for sinners Jesus bore the full brunt of the judgement upon sin. By this means the Lord fulfilled the words of 36:23: 'I will show the holiness of my great name, which has been profaned among the nations, the name you have profaned among them.'

No one can say that the cross did not portray God's holy hatred of sin. Yet it also meant that the Lord was free to forgive sinners, for their sins had been judged in the death of Christ for them. Now he could justifiably go to the nations and fulfil the promises of 36:24–32. On the cross Jesus had died for the sins of the world; but because he was sinless himself death had no hold upon him and God raised him from the dead, setting him at his right hand in the position of lordship. Then on the Day of Pentecost the risen Lord Jesus Christ, having received from the Father the promised Spirit, poured him forth upon his people (Acts 2:33). Since that day millions of people, whose sins have been removed through the death of Christ, have received that same Spirit. He has taken out their hearts of stone and replaced them with hearts of living flesh, sensitive to the movings of God. Such people then follow God's decrees and are careful to keep his laws, not from threat of punishment or fear of failure, but through Spirit-implanted inner desires. We now want to do God's will. So 36:26,27 are still being fulfilled: 'I will give you a new heart and put a new spirit in you; I will remove from you your heart of stone and give you a heart of flesh. And I will put my Spirit in you and move you to follow my decrees and be careful to keep my laws.'

The ultimate effect of God's gracious work is described in 36:31: 'Then you will remember your evil ways and wicked deeds, and you will loathe yourselves for your sins and detestable practices.' This may seem strange. We might expect that when men and women receive full and free forgiveness solely through the action of the Lord on the cross and through no merit of their own, they would be so busy welcoming the freedom they now enjoy that they would not give too much thought to their sins. But, in fact, the free sovereign grace of God produces far more consciousness of sin than all the threats of the law. When we see what it cost the Lord to save us and how much undeserved suffering he endured on our behalf, we begin to see ourselves and our sin in a totally new light. We become more ashamed of ourselves, not less. What we previously thought of as minor infringements of the moral code suddenly become the nails that held the Son of God to a Roman gibbet. Grace is much more awe-inspiring than judgement.

At this point most people who are not believers completely misunderstand the nature of the Christian life. Convinced as they usually are that Christianity is just one more of the world religions offering salvation through good works, they assume that someone calling himself a Christian is claiming a moral excellence above that of others. Not unnaturally people resent this claim. But this is a total misunderstanding of the gospel. Christians, in fact, are more conscious of the sinfulness of sin than any other group. They have seen their own moral need and fled to the cross of Christ as the only solution to that need. And that is only the beginning of an ever deeper realization of the sinfulness of sin, and an ever deeper gratitude to the Lord for dealing with it.

The Christian gospel is therefore more radical in its diagnosis of the world's need and more drastic in meeting it than any other alternative. Nothing short of a change of heart and a new spirit can fit humanity for God's new rule, and just such a new heart and spirit have been provided through the death and resurrection of Jesus

Christ and the coming of the Spirit. So those of us engaged in ministering the gospel of Jesus Christ do not have to be ashamed of what we are doing. We are not peddling an out-of-date ideology, but sharing the good news of the mighty grace of God, the only news that can make men and women new people through the power of the Spirit of God. A new world calls for a new people.

15.
A new people

Human life is like a pendulum. Fashions in music swing
from melodious to cacophanous; fashions in ladies' dress
fluctuate between long skirts and short. Morally men
and women move from asceticism to licence, from saying
nothing about sex to talking about nothing else. We find
it very hard to reach the medium between extremes.
When this swing happens in theology, however, we run
into dangerous trouble. We have seen how Ezekiel mourned
over the disintegration of his society; he had not opted
out of his generation. Yet he was also concerned for the
individual. Disintegration in society begins with the
individual, and so does restoration. This pendulum between
emphasis on the one and the many swings violently from
side to side, and from generation to generation. The
Christian community becomes caught up in this process.

In recent years Christians have divided strongly into
those committed to the reform of society and the intro-
duction of social justice, and those committed to the
salvation of the individual. One group quotes from Isaiah
61 as the classic basis for their crusade to free the captives
and bring justice to the poor. They emphasize the sinfulness of structures, as well as of the individual, and call
for the church to be involved in politics to change the
status quo. The other group points out that society will
not really change until people are changed, and that new
people should automatically move on to change the status
quo. The first group see the second as having their heads
in the clouds and put their finger on the injustices that

still flourish in communities with a high proportion of believers, even of those who claim to be born again. The second group accuse the first of financing Marxist revolution and point to the failure of reformed structures in countries where revolutions have taken place. People often seem to finish up worse off. Recently these two views have begun to move closer to each other, but they still divide Christians deeply.

Ezekiel had a profoundly pessimistic view of the ability of sinful human beings to produce a just society. He therefore saw the only hope in God's raising up his own supreme King, who will eventually come back to earth to rule. God also showed to Ezekiel the need for new people to inhabit the new world and be part of the new society. But that does not mean that Ezekiel endorsed individualism or saw no hope for a new community on earth. Chapter 37 makes clear that the new people of chapter 36 should be part of a new divine community which God would raise up on earth from the ruins of the old society. He may not have seen any hope of producing a Utopian society from the mass of mankind, but he did see God raising up a new pilot community to live as his people and to portray to the rest of the world a new God-orientated society.

The prelude to the new society

The Lord put his hand on Ezekiel, brought him out by his Spirit and conducted him round a cemetery. But this was no ordinary graveyard. For one thing, the bones lay about in confused heaps. They had been around for a long time, for they were very dry (37:1,2). Ezekiel saw in those bones a desolate picture of his own people. They could be written off. Formed to be the people of God, the pilot project of life as it should be lived, they had lost their way and finished up like everyone else, dead in more ways than one.

The Lord then asked him, 'Son of man, can these bones live?' Ezekiel answered very carefully. He knew enough about man not to be falsely optimistic, but he also knew enough about God to believe that all things are possible with him. So he behaved as a reverent agnostic and said, 'O Sovereign Lord, you alone know' (37:3). Some Christian leaders exude a baseless optimism, telling us of the ceaseless onward march of the gospel if we will only muster all our forces and get on with it. Ezekiel did not really know what was going to happen and was humble enough to say so. Reverent, God-honouring agnosticism can be a Christian virtue. Ezekiel was under no illusion about the difficulty of the job. Dead bones do not come to life easily and their dryness makes hope as brittle as the bones. Christian realism calls for honest acceptance of the truth of Ephesians 2:1 concerning human nature: 'You were dead in your transgressions and sins.' You do not produce a new society from people completely out of touch with God and oblivious of his presence, cheerfully content to live a life centred around self.

The producers of a new society

If men are dead they can hardly help themselves. So the Lord told Ezekiel that he himself intended to do something about it. He was going to make breath enter into those bones and they would come to life; he would make flesh come upon them and cover them with skin. The initiative and the action lay with him. Yet he also used a human instrument. Ezekiel had to prophesy to those bones and they had to hear the word of the Lord. Then God would come and bring life. Chapter 37:4—6 therefore makes plain, firstly, that man without God can produce no life at all and, secondly, that God does not normally choose to produce life without using man as his instrument.

The initiative still lies with God and always will. A popular definition of evangelism today insists on registered response as a necessary result. Unless you have secured that response you have not evangelized. You must not be content to preach the gospel, but must push on to make sure the person believes. Such a definition stems from a deep concern for people without Christ and a warm zeal for the glory of God. But it also stems from a faulty theology, for we cannot secure such a response. Unless God does his work in the heart of the hearer, we are not only incapable of securing the right response, but can in fact innoculate the person against the real thing. If we really think we can persuade people to believe, and that we must do so in order to fulfil our commission, then we finish up with the end justifying the means. If we do not obtain the right result, not only have we failed to obey the Lord's command, but the person himself has lost his opportunity to share in the benefits of the gospel. So we feel justified in manipulating hearers at evangelistic rallies through psychological, as well as spiritual pressures. Such tactics as soft music, often-repeated calls for decision, people primed to come out to the front to start the stream going, high emotional atmosphere and promises or warnings that 'This is your last opportunity' not only can, but really ought to be used. We must beg people to believe, to make their decision for the Christ we have offered to them. But we forget that basically the same motive led in former years to the Spanish Inquisition. The priests of those days were so sure that a soul who did not believe was lost eternally that they felt justified in using even torture to compel acceptance. If man is capable of making an unaided response to God, ultimately anything is justified.

The reverse side of this coin is a bland indifference that contents itself with a cold presentation of undigested truth, and blames the hearer for lack of response. This can sometimes be associated with a preoccupation with the finer points of orthodoxy and an almost complete disregard of the unevangelized world outside. Some of us believe so firmly in the sovereignty of God and the glories of Reformed theology that we forget there are two billion people as yet unreached by the gospel. Ezekiel was sent to a cemetery, but he was sent. Those bones could never have lived if he had sat in his refugee camp debating the furniture of the temple. No one could have accused a man like George Whitefield of either extreme. He preached the gospel earnestly, but he never manipulated people. He waited for the Lord to bring life to the dead bones around him, but he went.

I travel a great deal both around Asia and also in other parts of the world. Everywhere I see some glorious works of God. But I also see the pathetic influence of shallow evangelism that makes no deep impact on the roots of a person's life and litters the scene with half-nourished people, who have not so much as heard if there be a Holy Spirit, let alone experienced his creative power in their lives. I also find churches that mourn this state of affairs and pride themselves on their orthodox theology, but which have not sent a missionary for thirty or more years and do not seem to see any need to do so. We cannot complain about inadequate methods of evangelism unless we are prepared to go and do it differently ourselves. We need a firm conviction of the power of the gospel to bring life through the work of the Holy Spirit, without whom we can do nothing; and we also need a zealous concern to get out into the vast cemetery-like communities of our world and bring that message to them.

The means of producing the new society

God commanded Ezekiel to prophesy twice, once to the bones and then to the breath. The means of producing a new community in a world of spiritually dead people are the Word of God and the Spirit of God.

Firstly, the Lord told Ezekiel to prophesy to the dead bones and say, 'Dry bones, hear the word of the Lord!' (37:4.) Then he declared that he would bring them to life. We might feel that addressing a valley of dry bones and telling them to live is hardly a sane occupation. Anyone walking into a cemetery today and behaving like that would soon be escorted to a sympathetic counsellor, at best. Yet that is exactly what Ezekiel was told to do — and it is also exactly what we are told to do. Man without God is dead and as unresponsive to him as a corpse. Yet God has decreed that he intends to bring people to life simply through the preaching of his truth. We go to preach, as convinced as Ezekiel must have been that he had no power at all to make those bones live. But we also go in faith, believing that the same God who could bring life to Ezekiel's graveyard can bring life to spiritually dead people. In 2 Corinthians 4 Paul faced this same dilemma. First he made sure that there was nothing wrong with his preaching (verses 1,2), and then concluded that sometimes the gospel was still veiled in the minds of unbelieving people through the blinding activity of Satan (verses 3,4). That did not deter him from going on preaching, for in his hands was the gospel of the Creator God who on the Damascus road had shone his light into Paul's dark heart.

The other means of producing a new people is the Spirit of God. Just preaching a mere word could only take Ezekiel so far. When he had done it, all he had before him was a community of corpses, clothed in skin and flesh but lacking life. So the Lord told him to prophesy again, this time to the breath, saying, 'Come from the four winds, O breath, and breathe into these slain, that they may live' (37:9). When he did this, the breath entered into their bodies and they stood up like a vast army. Without the Spirit of God bringing the breath of his life into men and women, we preach and teach in vain. Orthodoxy in this connection can be as dead as liberalism. Indeed, it can be worse, for what should carry the power of life proves no more potent than any other remedy and convinces people that in fact the truth is powerless. When Paul preached, he did so with the power of the Holy Spirit and with deep conviction. He did not simply hurl concepts at his congregation, but he sought to move them, prayed that God would draw them and by his warmth convinced them that he was dealing with matters of life and death.

There is a great renewal of interest in power today. Whatever we may think of the charismatic movement, it has brought a new interest in the work of the Holy Spirit and a new desire for his working in human lives. Sometimes this has gone to extremes and instead of allying the Holy Spirit with the Word of God, people have developed an unhealthy reliance on special revelations, even to the extent of devaluing the place of the Word. But the Spirit works through the Word and his work is essential. Once again we must keep the two aspects in balance and not swing from one end of the pendulum to the other.

When Paul found some Christians in Ephesus, he was clear that something was wrong with them, for they failed to show any sign of the power of the Spirit of God in their lives (Acts 19:1–7). He was therefore rightly concerned to do something about it, and when he discovered that they knew nothing of the Holy Spirit he preached Jesus to them. He applied the truth of the Lord Jesus Christ to their hearts as the first step in remedying their need of the Spirit. So we need both the truth of God enshrined in his Word and the power of the Spirit to work through and with that Word in producing new life.

The pessimism that hinders the new society

Israel reacted to the judgement of God upon her with profound pessimism. Understandably, when your enemies have just flattened your walls, burnt your temple, raped your women, slaughtered your men and carried the rest of the population off into captivity, you are not bursting with hope. Ezekiel saw the people of Israel as saying, 'Our bones are dried up and our hope is gone; we are cut off' (37:11). The same people who had pinned their hopes on a false optimism now sank in the despair of a blank pessimism. They could see no hope at all. To them Ezekiel brought a message of hope: 'This is what the Sovereign Lord says: O my people, I am going to open your graves and bring you up from them . . . I will put my Spirit in you and you will live, and I will settle you in your own land. Then you will know that I the Lord have spoken, and I have done it, declares the Lord' (37:12–14).

The state of the church in some parts of the world today could easily provoke in Christians a state of despair. We look around and ask ourselves whether these dry bones can ever live again. Yet such a situation calls neither for false optimism nor dark disillusion, but positive trust in the purposes of God, the Word of God and the power of the Spirit of God to change everything and to bring new life again. Nor must we confuse numbers with health. Some churches in Asia burst their doors with people, hold several services every Sunday and rejoice in multitudes going to worship. Westerners coming into them can be forgiven for thinking that they have hit revival. But the test of life lies not in the number of flesh-covered bones that dwell in the congregation, but in the extent to which the life of the Spirit of God is coursing through living bodies, producing the fruit of the Spirit and overflowing into society around. Whether the bones be few or many, the need is the same and the remedy is the same.

Proclaiming the truth of God in the power of the Spirit of God under the control of the sovereign grace of God can and will effect a difference. Dead churches can and do live again; we dare not write them off as dead bones, too dry for hope. God still intends his church to become his pilot community within a world ignorant of his grace and oblivious to his presence.

The result of new life in the new society

Ezekiel traces the effect of new life in the old bones in 37:15–28. The first result is a new unity. For years, the twin kingdoms of Israel and Judah vied with each other for supremacy, but God says that he will take them with their new life and 'they will become one in my hand'. These verses may well apply to the literal peoples of Israel and Judah, although finding the descendants of the old northern kingdom today would be a very difficult task indeed. However that may be, I firmly believe that when the Spirit of God moves to revive his people he takes them in his hands and makes them one. Evangelical Christians have shied away from the artificial structural unity of denominations so desired by the leaders of institutional Christianity. Yet in doing so they have sometimes ignored the theme of unity altogether, priding themselves on their purity in isolation from each other and forgetting the scriptural command to endeavour to maintain the unity of the Spirit in the bond of peace. The power of the Spirit in new life breaks down barriers and draws people together, not in undiscriminating chumminess, but in true God-given oneness.

The second effect Ezekiel traces is a new purity that cleanses from the defilement of all man-made objects of worship and devotion, saving people from their sinful backsliding, cleansing them and constituting them the real people of God (37:23). Unity without purity papers over wide cracks; so called purity without unity smells of pretence. The third effect of the production of the new society comes in the form of a new God-consciousness, with the Lord seen to be dwelling among his people and the nations knowing that the Lord has made Israel holy (37:24–28).

So Ezekiel brings a new message of hope to a people devastated by the results of their own sinfulness. Their false self-confidence shattered by an act of judgement, they could easily conclude that God had nothing good to say to them. But Ezekiel in these chapters draws a picture not simply of isolated rays of light here and there, but of a programme and a kingdom that God is actively at work producing in the world. From the vantage-point of history, we can look back and see that God has been doing that for a great many years. We are a part of that movement and we have no reason to be ashamed of the hope that is in us. The Lord is bringing in his new King and his new kingdom, a renewed people with hearts that beat in tune with his Spirit, a new society through the ministry of the Word and of the Spirit. However dark the present outlook, chapter 37 calls us to go out in confidence that dead bones can and will live, by the grace of our God.

· 16.
The last battle

The realism of biblical truth comes out nowhere more
clearly than in the sudden change of theme that crashes
out of Ezekiel chapters 38 and 39. Just as we have become
used to a new brightness of hope that provides a silver
lining to the earlier clouds of judgement, the sky darkens
again and the clouds of war roll into view. The fact is that
evil is deeply rooted in the earth as we know it, and its
vicious nature continues to the very last. Nor is evil an
impersonal force or disease like cancer. Behind it all lies
personal malevolent power headed by Satan, the great
adversary of good and of God, and he is not prepared to
surrender without a final struggle.

Ezekiel is not alone in introducing this jarring note at
the penultimate point in his message. These chapters are
closely paralleled by Revelation chapter 20, which speaks
of Armageddon just before the New Jerusalem descends
from heaven and brings the everlasting presence of God
to his battered world. Indeed, I believe we need to interpret
the message of Ezekiel in the light of the clearer revelation
of John if we are to understand what he has to say for us.

Ezekiel 38 begins with the Lord's word against that
mysterious personality, Gog of the land of Magog, the
chief prince of Meshech and Tubal. Some would identify
his land in modern terms as Russia, with its present
atheistic leadership. That would be convenient, especially
for those of us threatened by the militant atheism and
military might of Communism today. Personally I remain
unconvinced and question whether the evidence for this

categorical identification amounts to proof or even much more than guesswork. The fact that John views the same last battle of good and evil in Revelation 20:7–10 as Satan deceiving 'the nations in the four corners of the earth' would appear to me to imply a universal gathering of evil forces of all kinds for one final attempt to overthrow God's will.

In Ezekiel, the Lord himself controls the whole scenario. He says to Gog, 'I will turn you around, put hooks in your jaws and bring you out with your whole army.' True, 'On that day thoughts will come into your mind and you will devise an evil scheme.' The enemy will imagine that he has it all worked out as a bright idea, but even in that God is totally in control. Gog gathers his hordes and descends upon an unsuspecting people dwelling in peace and living without protection. He sees this as his great opportunity to pounce and to plunder. Actually the Lord is gathering the forces of evil together in one final rebellion, only to discredit them completely and destroy them for ever. Just as Pharaoh's heart was hardened in order that the Lord might manifest his great power in delivering Israel, so Gog and his army gather to meet their final catastrophe at God's hands.

The ultimate destruction of the forces of evil in no way depends upon human forces. When Gog attacks, 'my hot anger will be aroused, declares the Sovereign Lord' (38:18). This is followed by a great earthquake, the overturning of mountains, internecine conflict among Gog's own forces and various judgements, some of which are reminiscent of the ten plagues of the Exodus (38:19–22). In fact the last battle is hardly a battle at all, but an uneven contest between the malignancy of evil powers and the glory of Almighty God. The ultimate result therefore is that 'I will show my greatness and my holiness, and I will make myself known in the sight of many nations. Then they will know that I am the Lord' (38:23). After

all the blasphemies of history, God's name is finally vindicated and shown to have been holy all the time. All are
compelled to admit his glory and to bow before him.

So in chapter 39 weapons are struck from Gog's hands
and his army is a total loss, suffering casualties which
take seven months to inter. The result is that 'I will make
known my holy name among my people Israel. I will no
longer let my holy name be profaned, and the nations
will know that I the Lord am the Holy One in Israel'
(39:7). In Revelation 20 fire comes down from heaven
and devours the forces of Satan and of Gog as they
surround the camp of God's people, the city that he
loves. The devil is thrown into the lake burning with
sulphur, where the beast and the false prophet are thrown
(Revelation 20:9,10). The whole incident is followed by
the last judgement at the great white throne. God is
clearly shown to be Lord in his universe, evil is finally
defeated and holiness reigns in justice.

It is, of course, possible that in Ezekiel and Revelation
we have two successive incidents, one related to the
people of Israel and the other related to the final defeat
of Satan. Certainly there are references in Ezekiel to the
land of Israel and to the nations being made aware why
her people had been in exile from the land through their
unfaithfulness. Indeed, the last verse of chapter 39 portrays
the Lord no longer hiding his face from them, 'for I will
pour out my Spirit on the house of Israel, declares the
Sovereign Lord' (39:29). On the other hand, references to
Gog attacking 'a land of unwalled villages . . . a peaceful
and unsuspecting people — all of them living without
walls and without gates and bars' (38:11) certainly does
not fit Israel's defensive preparedness today.

I have no wish to dogmatize and I am not writing a
commentary that requires detailed investigation of such
matters. The broad message, which is underlined in
Revelation, is plain. The system of evil in this world is

militantly orchestrated by malevolent spiritual powers. History records the struggle of those forces to disfigure and destroy God's good creation and especially the summit of that creation, humanity. At times it almost seems as though evil has triumphed, until God steps in and vindicates his truth and his will. The cross was Satan's masterstroke, when seemingly he had the Son of God and the Son of man totally in his power — only for God to produce the trump card of the resurrection that left the enemy helpless. Since then and, indeed, from all eternity, the end result has never been in doubt. But that does not mean that no more fighting remains. The last convulsion is the most dramatic, being the final death struggle of the devil and resulting in the complete overthrow of the whole system of evil.

In the second half of Ezekiel we have seen God's answer to man's failure: his new ruler, who reigns over people who have new hearts and are possessed by his Spirit and who are members of a new community, the Bride of Christ, his church. Ezekiel 38 and 39 tell us that despite all the enemy opposition to the emergence of such a people all over the world, and despite a final attempt to destroy them, Satan is a defeated foe. All that remains is for his weapons to be struck from his hands and for God to bring in his judgement and his kingdom and rule. After Armageddon, the new Jerusalem comes down out of heaven from God and a new heaven and new earth appear in which righteousness finally dwells (Revelation 21:1,2). To the coming of that new rule Ezekiel's final chapters now lead us. Meanwhile God's people should lift up their heads, for their redemption draws near. The crescendo of evil that fills the world around us does not indicate that God has lost control — only that history is moving towards its final climax.

17.
The coming glory

The final chapters of Ezekiel may not be light reading but they carry the message of hope to its climax, the return of the glory of the Lord to dwell among his people. They resound to some of the same tones as the last chapter of the book of Revelation. They express in the language of a priest the highest aspirations of the people of Israel and must have evoked from them a joyful response. We do not think as they thought, or clothe our hopes in their language, but once we extract the substance of their anticipation we can rejoice with them in what is to come.

Before we look at the main message of these chapters 40—48, we must consider whether they were ever intended to be interpreted literally. Ezekiel's temple has never yet been built. Does God ever intend that it should be? Will we one day see this temple erected in Jerusalem, or are we looking at the symbolic expression of deep hopes and anticipations that are fulfilled in other ways? Is Revelation 21 an expansion of these concepts and the final revelation of the same fulfilment of human hopes on a world-wide canvas?

I cannot really believe that Ezekiel's temple was ever intended to be erected, or that he ever thought in those terms. If that is so, then we may wonder why the vision came in this form; but when the Lord wanted to communicate the fulfilment of all things in a way that would be intelligible at that time, he naturally spoke to Ezekiel in priestly, cultic language. We need not therefore be surprised at the large amount of detail included. In fact, many of

Ezekiel's visions are recorded in immense detail, much of which we might feel was not strictly necessary to convey the message.

When the Lord gave Moses instructions for the tabernacle, he told him to get the people to bring an offering to the Lord. Then he commanded Moses to 'have them make a sanctuary for me, and I will dwell among them. Make this tabernacle and all its furnishings exactly like the pattern I will show you. Have them make . . .' (Exodus 25:8–10). Materials had to be gathered, and the tabernacle was to be made according to a revealed pattern. By contrast, the temple is already made when Ezekiel is summoned to see it and to examine its size and shape. He is never told to go and gather materials to erect the building, or how it is to be paid for. Rather, he sees something already in existence that carries a message within itself. This fundamental difference in outlook seems to be very important.

In this connection, it is interesting to note that very little is said about the furnishings of the Holy Place and the Most Holy Place. There is no reference to the sacred ark that figures so largely in the tabernacle. Only the table of shewbread in the Holy Place receives mention. While considerable detail goes into some of the descriptions, other parts of the temple are glossed over with little comment. There is no mention of the high priest, which is remarkable if the temple was to be built literally; but if the presence of the Lord himself replaces the need for the high priest in the symbolism of the vision, then it is understandable. Similarly, there is no Day of Atonement in the new temple, a remarkable omission if it is to be used by a restored Israel upon earth.

That leads me to a theological factor. Scripture and revelation move consistently from outward form and symbolic ritual to inner meaning and spiritual reality. In the Old Testament we have a physical people and a

promised land, a sacrificial system of animal sacrifice and
a law outside the people as a standard. Blessing is largely
conceived in earthly, material terms. In the New Testament we have a people of God, redeemed through the
sacrifice of Christ that fulfils all the symbolism of the
old cultus. The Spirit of God writes the law of God on
the hearts of his people and empowers them to fulfil it.
Blessing lies in eternal life, real restored relationship with
God and ultimately the timeless enjoyment of this in his
presence. I find it inconceivable that the Lord intends any
of his people to return to a system of animal sacrifice.
When Christ, the one full and sufficient sacrifice, has been
offered once and for all, for what purpose would God
countenance a return to a superseded symbolism?

The measurements of Ezekiel's temple and its
surroundings raise further questions. The temple itself is
larger in area than that occupied by the entire city of
Jerusalem before the Exile, and the new city in these
chapters covers almost the whole of Judea west of the
Jordan. Even if the geography of Palestine were to be
altered by some atomic upheaval, the existence of such
a city and temple in this part of the earth stretches our
credulity. When the land is divided in chapters 47 and 48,
there is very little left of Palestine to use. And if there
were sufficient for the twelve tribes to have their allot-
ment, is it really feasible to divide the twelve tribes
literally, each to their own inheritance, after so many
hundreds of years of intermingling? Also, the divisions
in chapter 48 are very arbitrary; meaningful if symbolic,
but of questionable value if literal. No account is taken
of differing numbers among the tribes. Another problem
in a literal interpretation is the river that flows out from
inside the temple. The water comes out from under the
south side of the altar and rises to a rolling river in no
time at all. The trees on its banks provide fruit for food
and leaves for healing. Such a river we can conceive in

symbolism, and the symbols are glorious, as we shall see, but is such a mighty stream likely to be found literally in the middle of the temple? Is the temple built on the stream, or does the stream appear miraculously after the temple is built? I may, of course, be accused of lack of faith, but the parallels between this stream and the one in Revelation 21 are so strong that I feel believing reason requires us to look for symbolic meaning in these chapters rather than for some literal fulfilment.

One further observation points in the same direction. After Moses had set up the original tabernacle, carefully erected according to the detailed instructions of the Lord, 'the cloud covered the Tent of Meeting, and the glory of the Lord filled the Tabernacle' (Exodus 40:34). In Ezekiel 43, the glory of the Lord returns to the temple in the course of the same series of visions in which Ezekiel sees the dimensions and characteristics of the temple. In other words, the coming of the glory is a part of the vision, not a subsequent return on completion of the building. This would indicate that the Lord is giving a symbolic view of the return of his presence to dwell among his people, rather than foretelling what would happen when such a temple is built.

If in fact Ezekiel's temple was never intended to be erected (and indeed none of the rabbis of Israel ever suggested that it would be), we are at liberty to look for the message contained in this remarkable series of visions. We find the language strange indeed. Probably nothing is further from the comprehension of modern secular man than the geography of holiness expressed in the architecture of a temple and the elaborate descriptions of a sacrificial system he finds confusing and unnecessary. Yet the message is very clear and much needed today.

The need for holiness

The first and most vital emphasis is the necessity of holiness, without which 'no one will see the Lord' (Hebrews 12:14). Israel had failed miserably in maintaining a distinction between that which is common and unclean and that which is holy, despite all the regulations of her sacrificial system. Ezekiel had complained against her leaders that they 'do not distinguish between the holy and the common; they teach that there is no difference between the clean and the unclean; they shut their eyes to the keeping of my Sabbaths, so that I am profaned among them' (22:26). God's glory had removed from their temple for that very reason, and he would only return when holiness had been restored. In Israel, as in modern secular society, there was very little sense of awe. Everyone was on the same level in their own thinking and the old barriers were seen as outdated. Instead, therefore, of lifting people to new heights, society reduced everything to a monotonous plain of common mediocrity. In the new temple, Ezekiel sees God reversing this whole trend and exalting his glory above everything.

The temple itself is built on the basis of separation, with wide open spaces between various sections and particularly between the common life of the people and the temple building itself. A sense of distance prevails. In 42:20 we read of a wall around the temple 243 feet long and equally wide 'to separate the holy from the common'. The same chapter speaks of 'the most holy offerings – the grain offerings, the sin offerings and the guilt offerings – for the place is holy' (42:13). The surrounding area on top of the mountain is also to be 'most holy. Such is the law of the temple' (43:12). The people of Israel in this same place are to be ashamed of their sins when the temple is described to them. They are to consider its plan, and if they are ashamed of all they have done Ezekiel is to 'make known to them the design of the temple . . . so that they may be faithful to its design and follow all its regulations' (43:10,11). This does not necessarily imply that the temple was to be made, but it does show that the message of holiness conveyed by the design must be indelibly printed on the minds of God's people.

Holiness is little talked about today, for much the same reason as it was little valued in Jerusalem then. There has to be a restored view of holiness before the Lord will return in glory to his people. That is the message of Ezekiel. Holiness is often misunderstood as either a list of artificial rules and regulations, or an unmanly pious mysticism that few people want to follow. In fact, in the Word of God it is a strong positive concept of pure and practical Christian living, perfectly portrayed in the life of Jesus Christ. We find the same emphasis on holiness in the new Jerusalem that John saw coming down out of heaven (Revelation 21:2), for this is the 'Holy City'. We tend to associate cities with all that is worst in human nature — disintegration, disease, crime and vice. But the holy city to come excludes from its gates 'the cowardly, the unbelieving, the vile, the murderers, the sexually immoral, those who practise magic arts, the idolaters and all liars' (Revelation 21:8). The hope for our world is holiness, and in an era when more and more people crowd into the cities, we can be thankful that God's promises for his coming kingdom are embodied in the picture of a holy city that comes down from himself and from which all evil has been obliterated. Ezekiel saw this truth thousands of years ago.

The river of blessing

A second main emphasis of these visions comes in the

picture of the river that flows from the temple in chapter 47, one of the few parts of Ezekiel with which most people are familiar. The river flows from the south side of the altar and out under the south side of the temple, and grows rapidly deeper as it progresses. It then flows into the Dead Sea and brings life wherever it goes, freshening the water, producing all kinds of fish and providing water for endless trees to line its banks and produce fruit for food and leaves for healing (47:1–12).

Water is life in the Scriptures. Any Israelite would know only too well the vital necessity of water, after experiencing its lack so many times. This river of life flows from the place of sacrifice and reconciliation and produces life wherever it goes. No more will Israel be dependent upon the uncertain provision of the rains to water her crops. The river flows in the most unfruitful area of all, sweetening even the Dead Sea. No one could miss the meaning of this: the blessing of God brought to his people through sacrifice and freely flowing out to bring life and healing. No picture could more adequately express what the Lord wanted to convey also through John. So in the new Jerusalem of Revelation 22 the angel shows John 'the river of the water of life, as clear as crystal, flowing from the throne of God and of the Lamb down the middle of the great street of the city'. Once again the trees on its banks give fruit for food and leaves for healing, this time not only to Israel but to all the nations (Revelation 22:1,2).

God's ultimate purposes for mankind are all perfect. He has provided a stream of life that flows from the cross of Calvary to be the water of life to a thirsty people and to bring healing from sin and sustenance through this world. In his final provision the river of the water of life still flows from the Lamb, but now he is seated upon the throne. Yet he still says, 'Whoever is thirsty, let him come; and whoever wishes, let him take the free gift of the water of life' (Revelation 22:17).

The presence of God

Above all else, the temple of Ezekiel's visions is the place
to which the glory of God can and does return. Grieved
by the awful apostasy of his people, the Lord was seen
in chapters 10 and 11 withdrawing gradually from his
temple, leaving the city to its fate. In chapter 43 the
glory returns to the new temple, coming in from the
east as it had withdrawn to the east. It is the same vision
of the glory of God that we saw in chapter 1 and subse-
quently the vision Ezekiel had seen when the Lord 'came
to destroy the city'. The new temple has been purged of
all the evil and the Lord now says, 'This is where I will
live among the Israelites for ever' (43:7). The Lord is
exactly the same; he never changes in all his glory and
transcendence. But he can only live among his people
when they have been purified and cleansed and will live
according to his will.

Similarly, the climax of the book of Revelation is
the holy city of chapter 21, where a loud voice from the
throne says, 'Now the dwelling of God is with men, and
he will live with them. They will be his people, and God
himself will be with them and be their God. He will wipe
every tear from their eyes. There will be no more death
or mourning or crying or pain, for the old order of things
has passed away' (Revelation 21:3,4). The presence of
God among his people is their ultimate hope; nothing can
exceed that in blessing and glory. What Adam lost in the
Garden of Eden was the presence of God communing
with him in the cool of the day. Ever since that time
mankind has been disorientated in this world, seeking
in vain to live an autonomous life apart from the God
who made him and loves him. Yet all through history
the Lord has been working towards that glorious day
when sin has not only been dealt with through the cross,
but its very presence has been eliminated from God's
world.

In Ezekiel there is no high priest, but a much enlarged temple, filled with the presence of God himself. In Revelation there is no temple at all, and indeed none is needed, 'because the Lord God Almighty and the Lamb are its temple' (Revelation 21:22). The presence of God in the new Jerusalem fills the whole city, not only replacing the temple but providing all the light that is needed. In other words, the whole city is holy and not just one particular part. The great reversal has taken place. We have reduced everything to a sordid secularity with nothing considered holy, but the Lord will one day come to set up a totally holy society, where he may dwell with his people because nothing can defile. In Ezekiel, the temple is restricted to the people of Israel, but in Revelation there is constant reference to the kings of the earth bringing their splendour in, to the glory and honour of the nations being brought into it and to the river being available for the healing of the nations. The people of God are no longer limited to one people, for through the death of Jesus Christ salvation has been made available to all. But the message of Ezekiel and of Revelation is still basically the same. Only when God dwells with mankind can we look for the final solution to our problems, and that day will certainly come.

So these visions of the new temple crown the silver lining that permeates and shines through the second half of Ezekiel's prophecies. The coming of the new ruler to reign over a new and purified people, who are filled with his Spirit and united in a common body across the deepest divide of history, is crowned by the return of the glory of the Lord to live among his people for ever. He will provide for their deepest needs through the river of life that flows from his altar and throne. The godlessness and apostasy of our society may be as depressing as in Ezekiel's day. We know that our society, like his, is under judgement unless something happens to turn us round; but we must not allow the cloud to dominate our thinking. In the gospel we have the message of a new ruler, a new heart, a new people and a new hope. God has promised to shine through the clouds and ultimately to accomplish all his purposes of grace. The malignant forces that oppose us will one day be destroyed, and God will bring in his King and his kingdom. That hope can hardly be better expressed than by the simple words with which Ezekiel finishes his account of the new temple and his book as well: 'THE LORD IS THERE.'

Other books by

DENIS LANE

published by Evangelical Press

A Man and his God

The Christian and the life of faith

'If only I had more faith!' is a cry from the heart of many Christians. There are times of disillusionment, times when faith seems beyond our grasp, times when faith has not come up to our expectations.

Too often Christians impart to faith a magical quality that it was never meant to have. It is not a wand to wave over life in order that problems and difficulties may disappear.

True faith is a living link with God that affects every area of our life. Such faith is clearly exemplified in the life of Abraham. Here we see what the true relationship should be between 'A Man and his God'.

"The message of the book is vital–it aims to clarify the average Christian's concept of faith and stimulate new confidence in the eternal God."

Christian Herald

Preach the Word

Too little of contemporary preaching is really an exposition of what the Word of God actually says. Sincere exhortation and a fund of good stories are no substitute for the convincing power and authority of the Word of God.

The object of this book is not only to call preachers back to the preaching of the Word, but also to give definite instruction in sermon preparation and presentation. It will be profitable, not only for full-time pastors, but also for those preparing for the ministry and those already engaged in lay preaching.